MW00447008

Verse by Verse Commentary on the Book of

ROMANS

Enduring Word Commentary Series
By David Guzik

The grass withers, the flower fades,
but the word of our God stands forever.
Isaiah 40:8

Commentary on Romans

Copyright © 2002 by David Guzik

Printed in the United States of America

ISBN 1-56599-041-2

Enduring Word Media

23 West Easy Street, #204

Simi Valley, CA 93065

Phone (805) 527-0199

Fax (805) 577-0388

Electronic Mail: ewm@enduringword.com

Internet Home Page: www.enduringword.com

Scripture references, unless noted, are from the New King James Version of the Bible, copyright © 1979, 1980, 1982, Thomas Nelson, Inc., Publisher.

Table of Contents

*For Our Son
Nathan*

Romans 1 - The Human Race Guilty Before God

A. The importance and impact of Paul's Letter to the Romans.

1. In the summer of 386, a young man wept in the backyard of a friend. He knew his life of sin and rebellion against God left him empty and feeling dead; but he just couldn't find the strength to make a final, real decision for Jesus Christ. As he sat, he heard children playing a game and they called out to each other these words: "Take up and read! Take up and read!" Thinking God had a message to him in the words of the children, he picked up a scroll laying nearby and began to read: *not in reveling and drunkenness, not in debauchery and licentiousness, not in quarreling and jealousy. But put on the Lord Jesus Christ and make no provision for the flesh, to gratify its desires* (Romans 13:13b-14). He didn't read any further; he didn't have to. Through the power of God's Word, Augustine gained the faith to give his whole life to Jesus Christ at that moment.

2. In August of 1513, a monk lectured on the Book of Psalms to seminary students, but his inner life was nothing but turmoil. In his studies he came across Psalm 31:1: *In Thy righteousness deliver me*. The passage confused Luther; how could God's *righteousness* do anything but condemn him to hell as a righteous punishment for his sins? Luther kept thinking about Romans 1:17, which says, *the righteousness of God is revealed through faith for faith; as it is written, "He who through faith is righteous shall live."* The monk went on to say: "Night and day I pondered until . . . I grasped the truth that the righteousness of God is that righteousness whereby, through grace and sheer mercy, he justifies us by faith. Therefore I felt myself to be reborn and to have gone through open doors into paradise . . . This passage of Paul became to me a gateway into heaven." Martin Luther was born again, and the Reformation began in his heart.

3. In May of 1738, a failed minister and missionary reluctantly went to a small Bible study where someone read aloud from Martin Luther's Commentary on Romans. As the failed missionary said later: "While he was describing the change which God works in the heart through faith in Christ, I felt my heart strangely warmed. I felt I did trust in Christ, Christ alone, for my salvation, and an

assurance was given me that he had taken *my* sins away, even *mine*." John Wesley was saved that night in London.

4. Consider the testimony of these men regarding Romans:

a. Martin Luther praised Romans: "It is the chief part of the New Testament and the perfect gospel . . . the absolute epitome of the gospel."

b. Luther's successor Philip Melancthon called Romans, "The compendium of Christian doctrine."

c. John Calvin said of the Book of Romans, "When anyone understands this Epistle, he has a passage opened to him to the understanding of the whole Scripture."

d. Samuel Coleridge, English poet and literary critic said Paul's letter to the Romans is "The most profound work in existence."

e. Frederick Godet, 19th Century Swiss theologian called the Book of Romans "The cathedral of the Christian faith."

f. G. Campbell Morgan said Romans was "the most pessimistic page of literature upon which your eyes ever rested" and at the same time, "the most optimistic poem to which your ears ever listened."

g. Richard Lenski wrote that the Book of Romans is "beyond question the most dynamic of all New Testament letters even as it was written at the climax of Paul's apostolic career."

5. We should also remember the Apostle Peter's words about Paul's letters: *Also our beloved brother Paul, according to the wisdom given to him, has written to you, as also in all his epistles . . . in which are some things hard to understand* (2 Peter 3:15-16).

a. The Book of Romans has life changing truth but it must be approached with effort and determination to understand what the Holy Spirit said through the Apostle Paul.

B. Introduction.

1. (1) Paul introduces himself to the Roman Christians.

Paul, a bondservant of Jesus Christ, called *to be* an apostle, separated to the gospel of God

a. **Paul**: The life and ministry of the Apostle Paul (also known as Saul of Tarsus) is well documented in Acts chapters 8 through 28, as well as Galatians 1 and 2, and 2 Corinthians 11 and 12.

i. It is almost universally agreed that Paul wrote Romans from the city of Corinth as he wintered there on his third missionary journey as described in Acts 20:2-3. This is based on Romans 16:1 and 16:23 along with 1 Corinthians 1:14. A variety of commentators pick the date of writing anywhere from 53 to 58 A.D.

ii. When Paul wrote the Book of Romans, he had been a Christian preacher for some 20 years. On his way to Jerusalem, he had three months in Corinth without any pressing duties. He perhaps thought this was a good time to write ahead to the Christians in Rome, a church he planned to visit after the trip to Jerusalem.

iii. As Paul endeavored to go to Rome, the Holy Spirit warned him about the peril awaiting him in Jerusalem (Acts 21:10-14). What if he were unable to make it to Rome? Then he must write them a letter so comprehensive that the Christians in Rome had the gospel Paul preached, even if Paul himself were not able to visit them.

iv. Because of all this, Romans is different than many of the other letters Paul wrote churches. Other New Testament letters focus more on the church and its challenges and problems. The Letter to the Romans focuses more on God and His great plan of redemption.

v. We know the Letter to the Romans was prized by the Christians in Rome; Clement of Rome's letter in 96 A.D. shows great familiarity with Paul's letter. It may be that he memorized it and that the reading of it became a part of virtually every meeting of the Roman church. As well, many scholars (Bruce and Barclay among them) believe that an edited version of Romans - without the personal references in Romans 16 - was distributed widely among early churches as a summary of apostolic doctrine.

b. **A bondservant . . . an apostle**: Paul's self-identification is important. He is *first* a **servant of Jesus Christ**, and *second* **called to be an apostle**.

i. There were several ancient Greek words used to designate a slave, but the idea behind the word for **servant** (*doulos*) is "complete and utter devotion, not the abjectness which was the normal condition of the slave." (Morris)

ii. "*A servant of Jesus Christ*, is a higher title than monarch of the world." (Poole)

c. **Separated to the gospel of God**: The idea of being an **apostle** is that you are a special ambassador or messenger. Paul's message is **the gospel** (good news) **of God**. It is **the gospel of God** in the sense that it belongs to God in heaven. This isn't a gospel Paul made up; he simply is a *messenger* of God's gospel.

i. **Separated unto the gospel**: "St. Paul may here refer to his former state as a *Pharisee*, which literally signifies a *separatist*, or one *separated*. *Before* he was separated unto the service of his own *sect*; *now* he is separated unto the Gospel of God." (Clarke)

ii. "Some think he alludes to the name of Pharisee, which is from separating: when he was a Pharisee, he was separated to the law of God; and now, being a Christian, he was separated to the gospel of God." (Poole)

d. **The gospel of God**: Other New Testament letters focus more on the church and its challenges and problems; Romans focuses more on **God**. "*God* is the most important word in this epistle. Romans is a book about God. No topic is treated with anything like the frequency of God. Everything Paul touches in this letter he relates to God. In our concern to understand what the apostle is saying about righteousness, justification, and the like we ought not to overlook his tremendous concentration on God." (Morris)

i. The word "**God**" occurs 153 times in Romans; an average of once every 46 words - this is more frequently than any other New Testament book. In comparison, note the frequency of other words used in Romans: *law* (72), *Christ* (65), *sin* (48), *Lord* (43), and *faith* (40). Romans deals with many different themes but as much as a book can be, it is a book about *God*.

ii. There are many important words in the vocabulary of Romans we must understand. Bruce quotes Tyndale's preface to Romans: "First we must mark diligently the manner of speaking of the apostle, and above all things know what Paul meaneth by these words - *the Law, Sin, Grace, Faith, Righteousness, Flesh, Spirit,* and such like - or else, read thou it ever so often, thou shall but lose thy labor."

2. (2-6) Paul introduces his gospel to the Romans.

Which He promised before through His prophets in the Holy Scriptures, concerning His Son Jesus Christ our Lord, who was born of the seed of David according to the flesh, *and* declared *to be* the Son of God with power according to the Spirit of holiness, by the resurrection from the dead. Through Him we have received grace and apostleship for obedience to the faith among all nations for His name, among whom you also are the called of Jesus Christ;

a. **He promised before through His prophets**: This gospel is not new, and it is not a clever invention of man. Paul's world was much like ours, with people liked "new" teachings and doctrines. Nevertheless, Paul didn't bring something new, but something very old in the plan of God.

b. **Concerning His Son Jesus Christ our Lord**: This is the center of Paul's gospel, the "sun" that everything this else orbits around. The center of Christianity is not a teaching or a moral system, it is a Person: **Jesus Christ**.

i. This Jesus has both a human origin (**born of the seed of David according to the flesh**), and an eternal existence (**declared to be the Son of God**). The evidence of Jesus' humanity is His human birth; the evidence of His deity is His **resurrection from the dead**.

ii. The resurrection of Jesus shows His divine power because He rose by His own power: *Destroy this temple and in three days I will raise it up again* (John 2:19).

iii. "There is a sense in which Jesus was the Son of God in weakness before the resurrection but the Son of God in power thereafter." (Morris)

c. **Declared**: This ancient Greek word (*horizo*) comes from the idea "to *bound, define, determine,* or *limit,* and hence our word *horizon,* the *line* that *determines* the farthest visible part of the earth in reference to the heavens. In this place the word signifies such a *manifest* and *complete exhibition* of the subject as to render it *indubitable.*" (Clarke)

d. **Jesus Christ our Lord**: It *means* something that the Apostle Paul called Jesus **Lord**: "This term could be no more than a polite form of address like our 'Sir.' But it could also be used of the deity one worships. The really significant background, though, is its use in the Greek translation of the Old Testament to render the divine name, Yahweh . . . Christians who used this as their Bible would be familiar with the term as equivalent to deity." (Morris)

e. **Through Him we have received grace and apostleship for obedience to the faith**: Paul's gospel impacts individual lives. It isn't interesting theory or philosophy, it is life-changing good news.

i. The gospel gave Paul and the church **grace and apostleship**, and one reason those two gifts were given was to produce **obedience to the faith**. "Without the GRACE, *favour,* and peculiar help of God, he could not have been an apostle." (Clarke)

ii. The gospel is big enough and great enough for the whole world; it must go out to impact **all nations**.

iii. The gospel had reached the Roman Christians, demonstrating that they **are the called of Jesus Christ**.

3. (7-15) Paul's desire to come to Rome.

To all who are in Rome, beloved of God, called *to be* saints: Grace to you and peace from God our Father and the Lord Jesus Christ. First, I thank my God through Jesus Christ for you all, that your faith is spoken of throughout the whole world. For God is my witness, whom I serve with my spirit in the gospel of His Son, that without ceasing I

make mention of you always in my prayers, making request if, by some means, now at last I may find a way in the will of God to come to you. For I long to see you, that I may impart to you some spiritual gift, so that you may be established; that is, that I may be encouraged together with you by the mutual faith both of you and me. Now I do not want you to be unaware, brethren, that I often planned to come to you (but was hindered until now), that I might have some fruit among you also, just as among the other Gentiles. I am a debtor both to Greeks and to barbarians, both to wise and to unwise. So, as much as is in me, *I am* ready to preach the gospel to you who are in Rome also.

a. **To all who are in Rome**: Paul had never been to Rome, and he did not found the Roman church. This makes the Book of Romans different because most of Paul's letters were to churches he founded. It seems the church in Rome began somewhat spontaneously as Christians came to the great city of the Empire and settled there. There is also no Biblical or historical evidence that the Apostle Peter founded the church in Rome.

i. Acts 2:10 describes how there were people from Rome among the Jews present at the Day of Pentecost; so when they returned home, there was a Christian community in Rome. Beyond that, the origins of the church in Rome are somewhat obscure, but Christians continually migrated to Rome from all parts of the Empire. It shouldn't surprise us that a church started there spontaneously, without being directly planted by an apostle.

ii. Even so, through mutual acquaintances or through his travels, Paul knew many of the Christians in Rome by name because he mentions them in Romans 16. Even if Paul only knew many of the Roman Christian by acquaintance, he knew two things about them and every true Christian. He knew they were **beloved of God** and that they were **saints**.

iii. **Called to be saints**: "You notice that the words 'to be' are put in by the translators; but though they are supplied, they are not really necessary to the sense. These believers in Rome were 'called saints.' They were not called because they were saints; but they became saints through that calling." (Spurgeon)

b. **Grace to you and peace from God**: Paul formally addresses his readers with his familiar greeting, combining the Greek greeting of **grace** with the Jewish greeting of **peace**. This **grace and peace** is not the kind wish of a man; they are *gifts*, coming **from God our Father and the Lord Jesus Christ**.

c. **I thank my God through Jesus Christ for you all, that your faith is spoken of throughout the whole world**: Paul was thankful for the good reputation of the church in Rome. Because of its location, this church had a special visibility and opportunity to glorify Jesus throughout the Empire.

> i. These Christians had to be strong. "The Christians of Rome were unpopular - reputed to be 'enemies of the human race' and credited with such vices as incest and cannibalism. In large numbers, then, they became the victims of the imperial malevolence - and it is this persecution of Christians under Nero that traditionally forms the setting for Paul's martyrdom." (Bruce)

> ii. "The Romanists urge this place to prove Rome the mother church; but without reason: the church of Thessalonica had as high a eulogy: see 1 Thessalonians 1:8." (Poole)

d. **Without ceasing I make mention of you always in my prayers**: Paul wanted the Roman Christians to know he prayed for them, and praying for an opportunity to visit them (**I may find a way in the will of God to come to you**).

> i. "No wonder that they prospered so well when Paul always made mention of them in his prayers. Some churches would prosper better if some of you remembered them more in prayer." (Spurgeon)

> ii. **For God is my witness** is perhaps Paul's acknowledgment of how easy it is to *say* you will pray for someone, and then fail to do it. He wanted them to *know* that he really prayed.

e. **I may impart to you . . . that I may be encouraged**: Paul's desire to visit the church in Rome was not merely to *give* to them, but to *receive* as well, because Paul realized that in their **mutual faith** they had something to give to him.

f. **I often planned to come to you (but was hindered until now)**: For a long time, Paul wanted to visit Rome and was only hindered by external circumstances. Perhaps some enemies of Paul implied he was *afraid* to go to Rome and preach the gospel in the "major leagues," in the Empire's leading city.

g. **I am a debtor both to Greeks and to barbarians, both to wise and to unwise**: Paul recognized he had something of a debt to Rome. The Roman Empire brought world peace and order; they brought a common cultural, and an excellent transportation system to the world. Paul used all these in spreading the Gospel; so he can best repay this debt by giving Rome the good news of Jesus Christ.

i. Paul was a tireless evangelist, working all over the world because he believed he had a debt to pay, and he owed it to the whole world.

h. **I am ready**: Spurgeon wondered if Paul didn't use the words "**I am ready**" as his motto. Almost the first words out of his mouth when he was saved were, *"Lord, what do you want me to do?"* (Acts 9:6).

- Paul was ready to preach and to serve (Romans 1:15)
- Paul was ready to suffer (Acts 21:13)
- Paul was ready to do unpleasant work (2 Corinthians 10:6)
- Paul was ready to die (2 Timothy 4:6)

i. "A Moravian was about to be sent by Zinzendorf to preach in Greenland. He had never heard of it before; but his leader called him, and said, 'Brother, will you go to Greenland?' He answered, 'Yes, sir.' 'When will you go?' 'When my boots come home from the cobbler;' and he did go as soon as his boots came home. He wanted nothing else but just that pair of boots, and he was ready to go. Paul, not even waiting for his boots to come home from the cobbler, says, 'I am ready.' Oh, it is grand to find a man so little entangled that he can go where God would have him go, and can go at once." (Spurgeon)

i. **I am ready to preach the gospel to you who are in Rome also**: This is boldness talking. "Talk of your brave men, your great men, O world! Where in all history can you find one like Paul? Alexander, Caesar, Napoleon, marched with the protection of their armies to enforce their will upon men. Paul was eager to march with Christ alone to the center of this world's greatness entrenched under Satan with *the word of the cross*, which he himself says is *to the Jews, an offence; and to Gentiles, foolishness.*" (Newell)

i. Ironically - in the mystery of God's irony - when Paul did eventually get to Rome, he came as a shipwrecked prisoner.

ii. "I do not suppose that Paul guessed that he would be sent there at the government's expense, but he was. The Roman Empire had to find a ship for him, and a fit escort for him, too; and he entered the city as an ambassador in bonds. When our hearts are set on a thing, and we pray for it, God may grant us the blessing; but, it may be, in a way that we never looked for. You shall go to Rome, Paul; but you shall go in chains." (Spurgeon)

4. (16-17) Paul introduces the theme of his letter: the righteousness of God, as revealed in the gospel of Jesus Christ.

For I am not ashamed of the gospel of Christ, for it is the power of God to salvation for everyone who believes, for the Jew first and also for the Greek. For in it the righteousness of God is revealed from faith to faith; as it is written, "The just shall live by faith."

a. After his introduction, Paul introduces his "thesis statement" for his Letter to the Romans. Leon Morris says of Romans 1:16 and 17: "These two verses have an importance out of all proportion to their length."

b. **I am not ashamed of the gospel**: This reveals Paul's heart. In a sophisticated city like Rome, some might be embarrassed by a gospel centered on a crucified Jewish Savior and embraced by the lowest classes of people - but Paul is not **ashamed**.

c. **For it is the power of God to salvation for everyone who believes**: This is *why* Paul is not ashamed of a gospel centered on a crucified Savior. He knows that the gospel - the good news of Jesus Christ - has *inherent* **power**. We do not *give* it power, we only stop *hindering* the power of the gospel when we present it effectively.

> i. The gospel is certainly *news*, but it is more than information; it has an inherent power. "The gospel is not advice to people, suggesting that they lift themselves. It is power. It lifts them up. Paul does not say that the gospel brings power, but that it *is* power, and God's power at that." (Morris)

> ii. In particular, the city of Rome thought it knew all about **power**: "Power is the one thing that Rome boasted of the most. Greece might have its philosophy, but Rome had its power" (Wiersbe). Despite all their power, the Romans - like all men - were powerless to make themselves righteous before God. The ancient philosopher Seneca called Rome "a cesspool of iniquity" and the ancient writer Juvenal called it a "filthy sewer into which the dregs of the empire flood."

> iii. **For salvation**: In the Roman world of Paul's day, men looked for **salvation**. Philosophers knew that man was sick and needed help. Epictetus called his lecture room "the hospital for the sick soul." Epicurus called his teaching "the medicine of salvation." Seneca said that because men were so conscious of "their weakness and their inefficiency in necessary things" that all men were looking "towards salvation." Epictetus said that men were looking for a peace "not of Caesar's proclamation, but of God's." (Cited in Barclay)

> iv. The gospel's power to salvation comes to **everyone who believes**. God will not withhold salvation from the one **who believes**; but believing is the *only* requirement.

d. **For the Jew first and also for the Greek**: This is the pattern of the spread of the gospel, demonstrated both by the ministry of Jesus (Matthew 15:24) and the initial ministry of the disciples (Matthew 10:5-6).

> i. This means that the gospel was meant to go first to the *ethnic and cultural* **Jew**, and then to the *cultural* Greek. "At this time the word

Greek had lost its racial sense altogether. It did not mean a native of the country of Greece . . . [a Greek] was one who knew the culture and the mind of Greece." (Barclay)

e. For in it the righteousness of God is revealed: Simply, the gospel **reveals** the **righteousness of God**. This revelation of God's righteousness comes to those with **faith**, fulfilling Habakkuk 2:4: **The just** - that is, the justified ones - **shall live by faith.**

> i. It is essential to understand exactly what the **righteousness of God** revealed by the gospel is. It does not speak of the holy righteousness of God that *condemns* the guilty sinner, but of the God-kind of **righteousness** that is *given to* the sinner who puts their trust in Jesus Christ.

> ii. **Righteousness**: William Barclay explains the meaning of this ancient Greek word *dikaioo*, which means *I justify*, and is the root of *dikaioun* (**righteousness**): "All verbs in Greek which end in *oo* . . . always mean to *treat*, or *account* or *reckon* a person as something. If God justifies a sinner, it does not mean that he finds reasons to prove that he was right - far from it. It does not even mean, at this point, that he makes the sinner a good man. It means that *God treats the sinner as if he had not been a sinner at all.*"

> iii. "It was the happiest day in Luther's life when he discovered that 'God's Righteousness' as used in Romans means *God's verdict of righteousness upon the believer.*" (Lenski)

> iv. This declaration is even greater when we understand that this is the **righteousness of God** given to the believer. It is not the righteousness of even the most holy *man*, nor is it the righteousness of innocent Adam in Eden. It is God's righteousness. "The righteousness which is unto justification is one characterized by the perfection belonging to all that God is and does. It is a 'God-righteousness'." (Murray)

> v. This faith (trust) in Jesus Christ becomes the basis of life for those who are justified (declared righteous); truly, **the just shall live by faith**. They are not only *saved* by faith, but they **live by faith**.

f. From faith to faith: The idea behind this difficult phrase is probably "by faith from beginning to end." The NIV translates the phrase **from faith to faith** as *by faith from first to last*.

> i. "He saith not, from faith to works, or from works to faith; but *from faith to faith*, i.e. only by faith." (Poole)

> ii. "Perhaps what it conveys is the necessity of issuing a reminder to the believer that justifying faith is only the beginning of the Christians

life. The same attitude must govern him in his continuing experience as a child of God." (Harrison) This is an echo of Paul's message in Galatians 3:1-3.

C. Why man must be justified by faith: the guilt of the human race in general.

1. (18a) The greatest peril facing the human race: the wrath of God.

For the wrath of God is revealed from heaven

a. **For the wrath of God is revealed from heaven**: The idea is simple but sobering - God's wrath is revealed from heaven against the human race, and the human race *deserves* the wrath of God.

b. **The wrath of God**: We sometimes object to the idea of the **wrath of God** because we equate it with human anger, which is motivated by selfish personal reasons or by a desire for revenge. We must not forget that **the wrath of God** is completely *righteous* in character.

i. "It is unnecessary, and it weakens the biblical concept of the wrath of God, to deprive it of its emotional and affective character . . . to construe God's wrath as simply in his purpose to punish sin or to secure the connection between sin and misery is to equate wrath with its effects and virtually eliminate wrath as a movement within the mind of God. Wrath is the holy revulsion of God's being against that which is the contradiction of his holiness." (Murrary)

ii. In Romans 1:16, Paul spoke of *salvation* - but what are we saved *from*? First and foremost we are saved from **the wrath of God** that we righteously deserve. "Unless there is something to be saved from, there is no point in talking about salvation." (Morris)

c. **The wrath of God**: In this portion of the letter (Romans 1:18-3:20), Paul's goal is not to *proclaim* the good news, but to demonstrate the *absolute necessity* of the good news of salvation from God's righteous wrath.

i. The **wrath of God** is not revealed in the gospel, but in the facts of human experience.

2. (18b-23) Why the human race is guilty before God: demonstrations of our **ungodliness and unrighteousness**.

Against all ungodliness and unrighteousness of men, who suppress the truth in unrighteousness, because what may be known of God is manifest in them, for God has shown *it* to them. For since the creation of the world His invisible *attributes* are clearly seen, being understood by the things that are made, *even* His eternal power and Godhead, so that they are without excuse, because, although they knew God, they did not glorify *Him* as God, nor were thankful, but became futile in their thoughts, and their foolish hearts were darkened. Professing to be wise,

they became fools, and changed the glory of the incorruptible God into an image made like corruptible man; and birds and four-footed animals and creeping things.

a. **Ungodliness**: This refers to man's offenses against God. **Unrighteousness** refers to the sins of man against man.

b. **Who suppress the truth in unrighteousness**: Mankind does in fact **suppress the truth** of God. Every truth revealed to man by God has been fought against, disregarded, and deliberately obscured.

c. **His invisible attributes are clearly seen**: God shows us something of His **eternal power and** divine nature through **creation, by the things that are made**. He has given a *general revelation* that is obvious both in creation and within the mind and heart of man.

i. **Clearly seen**: The universal character of this revelation and the clarity of it leave man **without excuse** for rejecting it. "Men cannot charge God with hiding himself from them and thus excuse their irreligion and their immorality." (Lenski)

d. **Although they knew God, they did not glorify Him as God**: The problem is not that man did not know God, but that he *did* know Him - yet refused to **glorify Him as God**. Therefore, mankind is **without excuse**. Instead of glorifying God we transformed our idea of Him into forms and images more comfortable to our corrupt and darkened hearts.

i. "Will you kindly notice, that, according to my text, *knowledge is of no use if it does not lead to holy practice*? 'They knew God.' It was no good to them to know God, for 'they glorified him not as God.' So my theological friend over there, who knows so much that he can split hairs over doctrines, it does not matter what you think, or what you know, unless it leads you to glorify God, and to be thankful." (Spurgeon)

ii. We can't seem to resist the temptation to create God into his own corrupt image, or even in an image beneath us. Tragically, we inescapably become like the God we serve.

iii. It is absolutely essential that we constantly compare our own conception of God against the reality of who God is as revealed in His Word. We can also be guilty of worshipping a self-made God.

iv. **Image** in Romans 1:23 is the ancient Greek word *eikon*. It is a dangerous thing to change the **glory of the incorruptible God into an** *eikon* **(image)** of your own choosing.

e. **Nor were thankful**: Man's simple *ingratitude* against God is shocking. "I cannot say anything much worse of a man than that he is not thankful to those who have been his benefactors; and when you say that he is not

thankful to God, you have said about the worst thing you can say of him."
(Spurgeon)

> i. "But when you glorify God as God, and are thankful for everything
> - when you can take up a bit of bread and a cup of cold water, and say
> with the poor Puritan, 'What, all this, and Christ too?' - then are you
> happy, and you make others happy. A godly preacher, finding that all
> that there was for dinner was a potato and a herring, thanked God
> that he had ransacked sea and land to find food for his children. Such
> a sweet spirit breeds love to everybody, and makes a man go through
> the world cheerfully." (Spurgeon)

f. **Professing to be wise, they became fools**: Our rejection of God's
general revelation does not make us smarter or better. Instead, it makes
mankind **futile in their thoughts**, and makes our **foolish hearts darkened** - and we become **fools**.

> i. The fact is once a man rejects the truth of God in Jesus, he will fall
> for anything foolish, and trust far more feeble and fanciful systems
> than what he rejects from God.

> ii. This futility of thinking, darkening of the heart, and folly must be
> seen as one example of God's righteous *wrath* against those who re-
> ject what He reveals. Part of His judgment against us is allowing us to
> suffer the damage our sinful course leads to.

3. (24-32) The tragic result of human guilt before God.

**Therefore God also gave them up to uncleanness, in the lusts of their
hearts, to dishonor their bodies among themselves, who exchanged the
truth of God for the lie, and worshiped and served the creature rather
than the Creator, who is blessed forever. Amen. For this reason God
gave them up to vile passions. For even their women exchanged the
natural use for what is against nature. Likewise also the men, leaving
the natural use of the woman, burned in their lust for one another, men
with men committing what is shameful, and receiving in themselves
the penalty of their error which was due. And even as they did not like
to retain God in *their* knowledge, God gave them over to a debased
mind, to do those things which are not fitting; being filled with all
unrighteousness, sexual immorality, wickedness, covetousness, mali-
ciousness; full of envy, murder, strife, deceit, evil-mindedness; *they are*
whisperers, backbiters, haters of God, violent, proud, boasters, inven-
tors of evil things, disobedient to parents, undiscerning,
untrustworthy, unloving, unforgiving, unmerciful; who, knowing the
righteous judgment of God, that those who practice such things are
deserving of death, not only do the same but also approve of those who
practice them.**

a. **Therefore God also gave them up**: In His righteous wrath and judgment, God gives man up to the sin our evil hearts desire, allowing us to experience the self-destructive result of sin. This phrase is so important Paul repeats it three times in this passage.

i. Hosea 4:17 expresses the judgmental aspect of God "giving us up," leaving us to our own sin: *Ephraim is joined to idols, let him alone.*

ii. We make a mistake when we think that it is God's *mercy* or *kindness* that allows man to continue in sin. It is actually His *wrath* that allows us to go on destroying ourselves with sin.

b. **Who exchanged the truth of God for the lie**: In every rebellion and disobedience against God we exchange **the truth of God for the lie** of our own choosing, and set the **creature** before the **Creator**.

i. Paul uses the definite article - it is not *a lie*, but **the lie. The lie** is essentially idolatry - which puts us in the place of God. It is the lie *you will be like God* (Genesis 3:5).

c. **For this reason God gave them up to vile passions**: Paul wrote this from the city of Corinth, where every sort of sexual immorality and ritualistic prostitution was practiced freely. The terminology of Romans 1:24 refers to this combination of sexual immorality and idolatrous worship.

i. This begins a passage where Paul describes the sin and corruption of the pagan world with an amazing directness - so direct that Spurgeon thought this passage unfit for public reading. "This first chapter of the Epistle to the Romans is a dreadful portion of the Word of God. I should hardly like to read it all through aloud; it is not intended to be so used. Read it at home, and be startled at the awful vices of the Gentile world." (Spurgeon)

d. **For even their women exchanged the natural use**: Paul uses homosexuality - both in the female and the male expressions - as an example of God giving mankind over to uncleanness and lust.

i. Some say that the Bible nowhere condemns lesbian homosexuality, but the **likewise** of Romans 1:27 makes it clear that the sin of homosexuality condemned in Romans 1:27 is connected to the sin of women mentioned in Romans 1:26.

ii. Paul doesn't even use the normal words for **men** and **women** here; he uses the words for *male* and *female*, using categories that describe sexuality outside of human terms, because the type of sexual sin he describes is outside of human dignity.

iii. Paul categorizes the whole section under the idea of **vile passions** - unhealthy, unholy. Nevertheless, Paul lived in a culture that openly approved of homosexuality. Paul didn't write this to a culture that agreed with him.

iv. Paul wrote to a culture where homosexuality was accepted as a part of life for both men and women. For some 200 years, the men who ruled the Roman Empire openly practiced homosexuality often with young boys.

v. At times the Roman Empire specifically taxed approved homosexual prostitution and gave boy prostitutes a legal holiday. Legal marriage between same gender couples was recognized, and even some of the emperors married other men. At the very time Paul wrote, Nero was emperor. He took a boy named Sporus and had him castrated, then married him (with a full ceremony), brought him to the palace with a great procession, and made the boy his "wife." Later, Nero lived with another man, and Nero was the "wife."

vi. In modern culture, homosexual practice reflects the abandonment of giving **them up to uncleanness, in the lusts of their hearts, to dishonor their bodies among themselves**. Statistics tell us that on average 43% of homosexuals say they have had 500 or more sexual partners in their lifetime, and only 1% of homosexuals say they have had four or less sexual partners in their lifetime.

vii. According to the United States Department of Health and Human Services, 77% of homosexuals say they have met sexual partners in a city park; 62% in a homosexual bar, 61% in a theater, 31% in a public restroom. Only 28% of homosexuals said that they knew their partners for at least a week before participating in homosexual sex.

viii. Homosexuals often seem to specialize in anonymous sex with no emotional commitment. At one time, London AIDS clinics defined a woman as promiscuous if she had more than six partners in her lifetime. They gave up trying to apply a workable definition to male homosexuals when it became clear that they saw almost no homosexual men who had less than six sexual partners a year.

e. **Receiving in themselves the penalty of their error which was due**: Paul speaks of a **penalty** for homosexual conduct; homosexuality has within itself a penalty. This speaks of the generally self-destructive nature of sin; it often carries within itself it's own penalty.

i. Sometimes it is the penalty of disease, which is the consequence of violating nature's order. Sometimes it is the penalty of rebellion, resulting in spiritual emptiness and all it's ramifications. In this sense the term "gay" is wishful thinking. It sends a message that there is something essentially happy and carefree about the homosexual lifestyle - which there is not.

f. Again, this "freedom" to disobey should be seen as God's *judgment*, not His kindness; those who engage in such acts are **receiving in themselves the penalty of their error**.

g. As further judgment, God gives man **over to a debased mind**, so that things that are disgraceful and sickening are readily accepted and approved.

i. The word **debased** (or, *reprobate* in the KJV) originally meant "that which has not stood the test." It was used of coins that were below standard and therefore rejected. The idea is that since man did not "approve" to know God, they came to have an "unapproved" mind.

ii. "The human race put God to the test for the purpose of approving Him should He meet the specifications which it laid down for a God who would be to its liking, and finding that He did not meet those specifications, it refused to approve Him as the God to be worshipped, or have Him in its knowledge." (Wuest)

iii. **A debased mind**: Our rebellion against God is not only displayed in our *actions*, but in our *thinking*. We are genuinely "spiritually insane" in our rebellion against God.

h. The list in Romans 1:29-31 gives concrete examples of the kind of **things which are not fitting**. Notice how "socially acceptable" sins (such as **covetousness, envy** and pride) are included right along with "socially unacceptable" sins (such as murder and being unloving).

i. **Covetousness**: This word literally describes *the itch for more*.

ii. **Whisperers**: "Secret detractors; those who, under pretended secrecy, carry about accusations against their neighbours, whether true or false; blasting their reputation by clandestine tittle-tattle." (Clarke)

iii. **Envy**: Is this a small sin? Envy is so powerful that there is a sense in which it put Jesus on the cross. Pilate *knew that they had handed Him over because of envy* (Matthew 27:18).

iv. **Proud**: "They who are continually exalting themselves and depressing others; magnifying themselves at the expense of their neighbours; and wishing all men to receive their *sayings* as oracles." (Clarke)

i. Those who either **practice** or **approve** of these things are **worthy of death**; they are the worthy targets of the wrath of God.

j. Where does all this violence, immorality, cruelty and degradation come from? It happens when men abandon the true knowledge of God, and the state of society reflects God's judgment upon them for this.

Romans 2 - The Guilt of the Moralist and the Jew

A. God's judgment upon the morally educated.

1. (1-3) An indictment against the morally educated man.

Therefore you are inexcusable, O man, whoever you are who judge, for in whatever you judge another you condemn yourself; for you who judge practice the same things. But we know that the judgment of God is according to truth against those who practice such things. And do you think this, O man, you who judge those practicing such things, and doing the same, that you will escape the judgment of God?

a. **Therefore you are inexcusable, O man, whoever you are who judge**: In Romans 1, Paul pointed out the sin of the most notoriously guilty. He now speaks to those who are generally moral in their conduct. Paul assumes they are congratulating themselves that they are not like the people described in Romans 1.

i. A good example of this mind set is Jesus' illustration of the Pharisee and the Publican. If we take those figures from Jesus' parable, Paul spoke to the Publican in Romans 1 and now he addresses the Pharisee (Luke 18:10-14).

ii. Many among the Jewish people of Paul's day typified the moralist; but his words in Romans 2:1-16 seem to have a wider application. For example, there was Seneca, the Roman politician, moral teacher and the tutor of Nero. He would agree wholeheartedly with Paul regarding the morals of most pagans, but a man like Seneca would think, "I'm different from those immoral people."

iii. Many Christians admired Seneca and his strong stand for "morals" and "family values." "But too often he tolerated in himself vices not so different from those which he condemned in others - the most flagrant instance being his connivance at Nero's murder of his mother Agrippina." (Bruce)

b. **For in whatever you judge another you condemn yourself**: After gaining the agreement of the moralist in condemning the obvious sinner, now Paul turns the same argument upon the moralist himself. This is because at the end of it all, **you who judge practice the same things**.

i. As we judge another person, we point to a standard outside of our self - and that standard condemns everyone, not only the obvious sinner. "Since you know the justice of God, as evidenced by the fact that you are judging others, you are without an excuse, because in the very act of judging you have condemned yourself." (Murray)

ii. **Practice the same things**: Notice that the moralist is not condemned for judging others but for being guilty of the same things that he judges others for. This is something the moral man would object to ("I'm not like them at all!"), but Paul will demonstrate this is true.

iii. Wuest, quoting Denney on **for you who judge practice the same things**: "Not, you do the identical actions, but your conduct is the same, i.e., you sin against light. The sin of the Jews was the same, but their sins were not."

c. **According to truth**: This has the idea of "according to the facts of the case." God will judge (and condemn) the moralist on the basis of the *facts*.

d. The point is made clear: if the moralist is just as guilty as the obvious sinner how will they **escape the judgment of God?**

i. **You** is emphatic in the question, "[do you think] **you will escape the judgment of God?**" Paul bears down here, letting his reader know that he is no exception to this principle. Paul knew how to get to the heart of his readers. "Our exhortations should be as forked arrows to stick in men's hearts; and not wound only, as other arrows." (Trapp)

ii. Lenski on the moralist: "Paul's object is far greater than merely to convict also them of unrighteousness. He robs them, absolutely must rob them, of their moralism and their moralizing because they regard this as the way of escape from God's wrath."

2. (4-5) God's judgment against the moralist is announced.

Or do you despise the riches of His goodness, forbearance, and longsuffering, not knowing that the goodness of God leads you to repentance? But in accordance with your hardness and your impenitent heart you are treasuring up for yourself wrath in the day of wrath and revelation of the righteous judgment of God,

a. **Or do you despise the riches of His goodness, forbearance, and longsuffering**: Paul points out that the moralist himself presumes upon the **goodness, forbearance, and longsuffering** of God, which all should bring the moralist into a humble repentance instead of an attitude of superiority.

i. **Goodness** may be considered God's kindness to us in regard to our *past* sin. He has been good to us because He has not judged us yet though we deserve it.

ii. **Forbearance** may be considered God's kindness to us in regard to our *present* sin. This very day - indeed, this very hour - we have fallen short of His glory, yet He holds back His judgment against us.

iii. **Longsuffering** may be considered God's kindness to us in regard to our *future* sin. He knows that we will sin tomorrow and the next day, yet He holds back His judgment against us.

iv. Considering all this, it is no surprise that Paul describes these three aspects of God's kindness to us as **riches**. The riches of God's mercy may be measured by four considerations:

- His *greatness* - to wrong a great man is a great wrong and God is greatest of all - yet He shows mercy
- His *omniscience* - if someone knew *all* our sin, would they show mercy? Yet God shows mercy
- His *power* - sometimes wrongs are not settled because they are out of our power, yet God is able to settle every wrong against Him - yet He is rich in mercy
- The *object* of His mercy: mere man - would we show mercy to an ant? Yet God is rich in mercy

v. Knowing how great God's kindness is, it is a great sin to presume upon the graciousness of God, and we easily come to believe that we *deserve* it.

b. **Forbearance and longsuffering**: Men of think of this as weakness in God. They say things like "If there is a God in heaven, let Him strike me dead!" When it doesn't happen, they will say, "See, I told you there was no God." Men misinterpret God's **forbearance and longsuffering** as His approval, and they refuse to repent.

i. "It seems to me that every morning when a man wakes up still impenitent, and finds himself out of hell, the sunlight seems to say, 'I shine on thee yet another day, as that in this day thou mayest repent.' When your bed receives you at night I think it seems to say, 'I will give you another night's rest, that you may live to turn from your sins and trust in Jesus.' Every mouthful of bread that comes to the table says, 'I have to support your body that still you may have space for repentance.' Every time you open the Bible the pages say, 'We speak with you that you may repent.' Every time you hear a sermon, if it be such a sermon as God would have us preach, it pleads with you to turn unto the Lord and live." (Spurgeon)

c. **Not knowing that the goodness of God leads you to repentance**: Many people misunderstand the **goodness of God** towards the wicked. They don't understand the entire reason for it is to lead them **to repentance**.

> i. Men should see the goodness of God and understand:

> - God has been better to them than they deserve
> - God has shown them kindness when they have ignored Him
> - God has shown them kindness when they have mocked Him
> - God is not a cruel master and they may safely surrender to Him
> - God is perfectly willing to forgive them
> - God should be served out of simple *gratitude*

> ii. Are you waiting for God to *drive* you to repentance? He doesn't work like that; God **leads you to repentance**. "Notice, dear friends, that the Lord does not drive you to repentance. Cain was driven away, as a fugitive and a vagabond, when he had killed his righteous brother Abel; Judas went and hanged himself, being driven by an anguish of remorse because of what he had done in betraying his Lord; but the sweetest and best repentance is that which comes, not by driving, but by drawing: 'The goodness of God leadeth thee to repentance.'" (Spurgeon)

> iii. "In the New Testament, repentance is not simply negative. It means turning to a new life in Christ, a life of active service to God. It should not be confused with remorse, which is a deep sorrow for sin but lacks the positive note in repentance." (Morris)

d. **You are treasuring up for yourself wrath in the day of wrath and revelation of the righteous judgment of God**: Because of this presumption on God's graciousness, Paul can rightly say that the moralist is **treasuring up . . . wrath in the day of wrath**.

> i. The moralist thinks he treasures up merit with God as he condemns the "sinners" around him. Actually, he only treasures up the **wrath** of God. "Just as men add to their treasure of wealth, so dost thou add to the treasures of punishment." (Poole)

> ii. As men treasure up the wrath of God against them, what holds back the flood of wrath? *God Himself!* He holds it back out of His **forbearance and longsuffering**! "The figure is that of a load that God bears, which men heap up more and more, making heavier and heavier. The wonder of it all is that God holds any of it up even for a

day; yet he holds up all its weight and does not let it crash down on the sinner's head." (Lenski)

e. **In the day of wrath and revelation of the righteous judgment of God**: In the first coming of Jesus the loving character of God was revealed with greatest emphasis. At the second coming of Jesus the righteous judgment of God will be revealed most clearly.

3. (6-10) God will judge the moralist because their works also fall short of God's perfect standard.

Who "will render to each one according to his deeds": eternal life to those who by patient continuance in doing good seek for glory, honor, and immortality; but to those who are self-seeking and do not obey the truth, but obey unrighteousness; indignation and wrath, tribulation and anguish, on every soul of man who does evil, of the Jew first and also of the Greek; but glory, honor, and peace to everyone who works what is good, to the Jew first and also to the Greek.

a. **Will render to each one according to his deeds**: This is an awesome and fearful thought, and it condemns the moralist as well as the obvious sinner.

b. **Eternal life to those**: If someone genuinely did good at all times, he could merit eternal life of his own accord - but there is none, because all, in some way or another are, have been, or will be **self-seeking and do not obey the truth, but obey unrighteousness**.

c. **Indignation and wrath, tribulation and anguish, on every soul of man who does evil**: Because all fall short of this standard of God's constant goodness, God's **wrath** will come to all who do evil - without respect to whether they are Jew or Gentile.

i. This judgment comes **to the Jew first**. If they are first in line for the gospel (Romans 1:16) and first in line for reward (Romans 2:10), then they are also first in line for judgment.

ii. The word **indignation** comes from the idea of "boiling up," thus having the sense of a passionate outburst. The word **wrath** comes from the idea of a swelling which eventually bursts, and applies more to an anger that proceeds from one's settled nature.

B. God's judgment upon the Jewish man.

1. (11-13) God's principle of impartiality.

For there is no partiality with God. For as many as have sinned without law will also perish without law, and as many as have sinned in the law will be judged by the law (for not the hearers of the law *are* just in the sight of God, but the doers of the law will be justified;

a. **For there is no partiality with God**: The word translated **partiality** comes from two ancient Greek words put together - *to receive* and *face*. It means to judge things on the basis of externals or preconceived notions.

i. Some ancient rabbis taught that God showed partiality towards the Jews. They said: "God will judge the Gentiles with one measure and the Jews with another."

b. **For not the hearers of the law are just in the sight of God, but the doers of the law will be justified**: God's righteous judgment is not withheld because someone has *heard* the law; it is only held back if someone actually *does* the law.

i. The Jewish person - or the religious person - may think that he is saved because he has the law; but has he kept it? The Gentile may think that he is saved because he does not have the law, but has he kept the dictates of his own conscience?

ii. "People will be condemned, not because they have the law or do not have the law, but because they have sinned." (Morris)

c. **As many as have sinned without law will also perish without law**: Judgment for sin can come with or without the law.

2. (14-16) Possession of the law is no advantage to the Jewish man in the Day of Judgment.

For when Gentiles, who do not have the law, by nature do the things in the law, these, although not having the law, are a law to themselves, who show the work of the law written in their hearts, their conscience also bearing witness, and between themselves *their* thoughts accusing or else excusing *them*) in the day when God will judge the secrets of men by Jesus Christ, according to my gospel.

a. **Although not having the law, are a law to themselves**: Paul explains why the Gentile can be condemned without the law. Their **conscience** (which is **the work of the law written in their hearts**) is enough to condemn them - or, theoretically this law on the heart is enough to justify them.

i. **Written in their hearts**: Many pagan authors of Paul's day referred to the "unwritten law" within man. They thought of it as something that pointed man to the right way. Though it is not embodied in written laws, it is in some ways more important than the written law.

ii. **A law to themselves** does *not* mean that these "obedient Gentiles" made up their own law (as we use the expression "a law unto himself"), but that they were obedient to **conscience**, the work of the law residing in themselves.

iii. "He indeed shows that ignorance is in vain pretended as an excuse by the Gentiles, since they prove by their own deeds that they have some rule of righteousness." (Calvin)

b. **Their thoughts accusing or else excusing them**: In theory, a man might be justified ("excused") by obeying his conscience. Unfortunately, every man has violated his conscience (God's internal revelation to man), just as every man has violated God's written revelation.

i. While Paul says in Romans 2:14 that a Gentile, may **by nature do the things contained in the law** he is careful to not say that a Gentile could *fulfill the requirements* of the law by nature.

ii. Though God has His *work* within every man (resulting in conscience), man can corrupt that work, so that conscience varies from person to person. We also know that our conscience can become damaged through sin and rebellion, but then can be restored in Jesus.

iii. If our conscience is condemning us wrongly, we can take comfort in the idea that *God is greater than our heart* (1 John 3:20).

c. **Their conscience also bearing witness**: People who have never heard God's word directly still have a moral compass they are accountable to - the **conscience**.

i. "God is describing how He has constituted all men: there is a 'work' within them, making them morally conscious." (Newell)

ii. "He is not saying that the law is written on their hearts, as people often say, but that the *work of the law*, what the law requires of people, is written there." (Morris)

d. **The day when God will judge**: On this day no man will escape God's judgment by claiming ignorance of His written revelation. Violating God's internal revelation is enough to condemn us all.

i. "God therefore will judge all nations according to the use and abuse they have made of this word, whether it was written in the *heart*, or written on tables of *stone*." (Clarke)

e. **According to my gospel**: Notice that the **day** of judgment was a part of Paul's **gospel**. He did not shrink from declaring man's absolute accountability to God.

i. " 'My gospel.' Does not this show his courage? As much as to say, 'I am not ashamed of the gospel of Christ: for it is the power of God onto salvation to every one that believeth.' He says, 'my gospel,' as a soldier speaks of 'my colors,' or of 'my king.' He resolves to bear this banner to victory, and to serve this royal truth even to the death." (Spurgeon)

f. God will judge the secrets of men by Jesus Christ: This concept is distinctively Christian. The Jews taught that God the Father alone would judge the world, committing judgment to no one - not even the Messiah.

3. (17-20) The boast of the Jewish man.

Indeed you are called a Jew, and rest on the law, and make your boast in God, and know *His* will, and approve the things that are excellent, being instructed out of the law, and are confident that you yourself are a guide to the blind, a light to those who are in darkness, an instructor of the foolish, a teacher of babes, having the form of knowledge and truth in the law.

a. **Indeed you are called a Jew, and rest on the law**: Every "boast" of the Jewish man in this passage concerns the possession of law. The Jewish people of Paul's day were extremely proud and confident in the fact that God gave His holy law to *them* as a nation. They believed this confirmed their status as a specially chosen people, and thus insured their salvation.

b. **Having the form of knowledge**: Although the Jew should gratefully receive the law as a gift from God, Paul will show how mere *possession* of the law justifies no one.

4. (21-24) The indictment against the Jewish man.

You, therefore, who teach another, do you not teach yourself? You who preach that a man should not steal, do you steal? You who say, "Do not commit adultery," do you commit adultery? You who abhor idols, do you rob temples? You who make your boast in the law, do you dishonor God through breaking the law? For "the name of God is blasphemed among the Gentiles because of you," as it is written.

a. **You, therefore, who teach another, do you not teach yourself?** It comes down to this principle: "You have the law, do you keep it? You can see how others break the law, do you see how you break it also?"

i. Much of the rabbinic Judaism of Paul's day interpreted the law so that they thought they were completely justified by the law. Jesus exposed the error of such interpretations (Matthew 5:19-48).

ii. God applies His law to both our *actions* and our *attitudes*. Sometimes we only want our attitudes evaluated, and sometimes only our actions. God will hold us accountable for both motives and actions.

iii. "Hypocrites can talk of religion, as if their tongues did run upon patterns, they are fair professors, but foul sinners; as was that carnal cardinal Cremensis, the pope's legate, sent hither, A.D. 1114, to interdict priests' marriages, and being taken in the act with a common strumpet, he excused it by saying he was no priest himself, but a corrector of them." (Trapp)

b. **You who abhor idols, do you rob temples**: Morris speaks to the idea of robbing temples. "Clearly some people held that a Jew might well make profits from dishonest practices connected with idolatry, and Paul may well have had this in mind."

c. **The name of God is blasphemed among the Gentiles because of you**: Paul reminds the Jew that God said in the Old Testament that the failure of the Jew to obey the law causes Gentiles to blaspheme God.

5. (25-29) The irrelevance of circumcision.

For circumcision is indeed profitable if you keep the law; but if you are a breaker of the law, your circumcision has become uncircumcision. Therefore, if an uncircumcised man keeps the righteous requirements of the law, will not his uncircumcision be counted as circumcision? And will not the physically uncircumcised, if he fulfills the law, judge you who, *even* with *your* written *code* and circumcision, *are* a transgressor of the law? For he is not a Jew who *is one* outwardly, nor *is* circumcision that which *is* outward in the flesh; but *he is* a Jew who *is one* inwardly; and circumcision *is that* of the heart, in the Spirit, not in the letter; whose praise *is* not from men but from God.

a. **For circumcision is indeed profitable if you keep the law**: Paul recognizes that a Jew may protest and say that his salvation is based on the fact that he is a descendant of Abraham, proven by **circumcision**. Paul rightly answers that this is irrelevant in regard to justification.

i. The Jew believed that his **circumcision** guaranteed his salvation. He might be *punished* in the world to come, but could never be *lost*.

ii. In Paul's day, some Rabbis taught that Abraham sat at the entrance of hell and made certain that none of his circumcised descendants went there. Some Rabbis also taught "God will judge the Gentiles with one measure and the Jews with another" and "All Israelites will have part in the world to come." (Barclay)

iii. **Circumcision** (or baptism - or any ritual in itself) doesn't save anyone. In the ancient world the Egyptians also circumcised their boys but it did not make them followers of the true God. Even in Abraham's day Ishmael (the son of the flesh) was circumcised, but it did not make him a son of the covenant.

iv. **Circumcision** and baptism do about the same thing that a label on a can does. If the outer label doesn't match with what is on the inside, something is wrong! If there are carrots inside the can, you can put a label that says "Peas" but it doesn't change what is inside the can. Being born again changes what is inside the can, and then you can put the appropriate label on the outside.

v. Of course, this is not a new thought. The Law of Moses itself teaches this principle: *Therefore circumcise the foreskin of your heart, and be stiff-necked no longer* (Deuteronomy 10:16).

b. **Therefore, if an uncircumcised man keeps the righteous requirements of the law**: If a Gentile were to keep the **righteous requirement of the law** through his conscience (as Romans 2:15 shows), would he not be justified, instead of the circumcised Jewish man who did not keep the law? The point is emphasized: *having* the law or *having* a ceremony isn't enough. God requires *righteousness*.

i. Morris quoting Manson: "If they are loyal to the good they know, they will be acceptable to God; but it is a very big 'if'."

c. **And will not the physically uncircumcised, if he fulfills the law, judge you who, even with your written code and circumcision, are a transgressor of the law?** This is God's answer to the one who says, "What about the Pygmy in Africa who has never heard the gospel?" God will judge that Pygmy by what he has heard, and how he has lived by it. Of course, this means that the Pygmy will be *guilty* before God, because no one has perfectly lived by their conscience, or perfectly responded to what we can know of God through creation.

i. The problem of the "innocent native" is that we can't find an *innocent* native anywhere.

ii. "What about the Pygmy in Africa who hasn't heard the gospel?" is a good question, but there are two far more important questions:

- What about you who hear the gospel, but reject it? What excuse is there for you?

- What about you, who are commanded to take the gospel to that Pygmy in Africa (Matthew 28:19), but refuse to do it?

d. **Whose praise is not from men but from God**: All the outward signs of religion may earn us praise **from men**, but they will not earn us praise **from God**. The evidence of our rightness with God is not contained in outward signs or works, and it is not assured because of our parentage. The evidence is found in the work of God in our heart which shows itself in fruit.

e. William Newell summarizes Romans 2 with "Seven Great Principles of God's Judgment" that are worth noting:

- God's judgment is **according to truth** (Romans 2:2)
- God's judgment is according to accumulated guilt (Romans 2:5)
- God's judgment is according to works (Romans 2:6)
- God's judgment is without partiality (Romans 2:11)

- God's judgment is according to performance, not knowledge (Romans 2:13)
- God's judgment reaches the secrets of the heart (Romans 2:16)
- God's judgment is according to reality, not religious profession (Romans 2:17-29)

Romans 3 - *Justified Freely by His Grace*

A. The righteousness of God's judgments.

1. (1-2) The advantage of the Jewish people.

What advantage then has the Jew, or what *is* the profit of circumcision? Much in every way! Chiefly because to them were committed the oracles of God.

a. **What advantage then has the Jew**: Paul has carefully explained in Romans 2 that the possession of the law or circumcision will not save a Jewish person. If this is the case, then what is the advantage of being "God's chosen nation"?

i. After all, if *there is no partiality with God* (Romans 2:11), what good is it to be Jewish?

b. **Much in every way!** Paul knows there are many advantages God gave to the Jewish people. In particular, He entrusted them with **the oracles of God**, which speaks of God's written revelation before the time of Jesus. He gave the Jewish people His Word, and that is an indescribable gift.

i. "This was their prime privilege, that they were God's library-keepers, that this heavenly treasure was concredited to them." (Trapp)

ii. Paul will later expand on the **advantage** of the Jewish people in Romans 9:4, explaining that Israel also had *the adoption, the glory, the covenants, the giving of the law, the service of God, and the promises.*

2. (3-4) Jewish unbelief does not make God wrong.

For what if some did not believe? Will their unbelief make the faithfulness of God without effect? Certainly not! Indeed, let God be true but every man a liar. As it is written: "That You may be justified in Your words, and may overcome when You are judged."

a. **For what if some did not believe?** The fact that the Jewish people as a whole to that point had rejected the gospel did not mean that God's faithfulness to them was in vain. It did not mean that God's work was futile or **without effect**.

> i. "I have to say, with Paul, 'What if some did not believe?' It is no new thing; for there have always been some who have rejected the revelation of God. What then? You and I had better go on believing, and testing for ourselves, and proving the faithfulness of God, and living upon Christ our Lord, even though we see another set of doubters, and another, and yet another *ad infinitu*m. The gospel is no failure, as many of us know." (Spurgeon)

b. **Certainly not! Indeed, let God be true but every man a liar**: Paul reminds us that God will be justified in all His actions. In the end, it will be demonstrated that even our unrighteousness somehow proclaimed His righteousness and glory, even if only in judgment.

> i. "Should any man say that the promise of God had failed toward him, let him examine his heart and his ways, and he will find that *he* has departed out of that way in which alone God could, consistent with his holiness and truth, fulfill the promise." (Clarke)

> ii. Spurgeon on **let God be true but every man a liar**: "It is a strange, strong expression; but it is none too strong. If God says one thing, and every man in the world says another, God is true, and all men are false. God speaks the truth, and cannot lie. God cannot change; his word, like himself, is immutable. We are to believe God's truth if nobody else believes it. The general consensus of opinion is nothing to a Christian. He believes God's word, and he thinks more of that than of the universal opinion of men."

3. (5) An objection regarding the unrighteousness of man and the righteousness of God.

But if our unrighteousness demonstrates the righteousness of God, what shall we say? *Is* **God unjust who inflicts wrath? (I speak as a man.)**

a. **But if our unrighteousness demonstrates the righteousness of God, what shall we say?** Paul brings the counter-argument of an opponent: "If my unrighteousness will demonstrate God's righteousness, how can God judge me? My sin ultimately serves to bring Him more glory, and that is good!"

b. **Is God unjust who inflicts wrath?** Paul was familiar with the line of thinking that says, "God is in control of everything. Even my evil will ultimately demonstrate His righteousness. Therefore God is **unjust** if He inflicts His **wrath** on me, because I'm just a pawn in His hand."

i. In theory, the most dramatic example of someone who might ask this question is Judas. Can you hear Judas make his case? "Lord, I know that I betrayed Jesus, but You used it for good. In fact, if I hadn't done what I did, Jesus wouldn't have gone to the cross at all. What I did even fulfilled the Scriptures. How can You judge me at all?" The answer to Judas might go like this: "Yes, God used your wickedness but it was still *your* wickedness. There was no good or pure motive in your heart at all. It is no credit to *you* that God brought good out of your evil. You stand guilty before God."

c. **I speak as a man**: This doesn't mean Paul is without the inspiration of the Holy Spirit and apostolic authority. Instead he explains that only as **a man** - a fallen man at that - would anyone dare to question God's justice.

4. (6-8) Paul's answer to the objection raised.

Certainly not! For then how will God judge the world? For if the truth of God has increased through my lie to His glory, why am I also still judged as a sinner? And *why* not *say*, "Let us do evil that good may come"?; as we are slanderously reported and as some affirm that we say. Their condemnation is just.

a. **Certainly not! For then how will God judge the world?** Paul dismisses the question of his opponent easily. If things were such as his opponent suggested, then God could judge *no one*.

i. It is true that God will use even the unrighteousness of man to accomplish His work and bring praise to His name - Judas' betrayal of Jesus is a perfect example. Nevertheless, part of the way God glorifies Himself in man's sin is by righteously *judging* that unrighteousness.

b. **How will God judge the world?** For both Paul and his readers it was a given that a judgment day was coming, when some will be acquitted and some condemned. He didn't need to contest this point; it was simply understood in that culture.

i. Paul understood that God would **judge the world**, both Jew and Gentile. Many of the Jews of Paul's day figured that God would condemn the Gentile *for* his sin, but save the Jew *despite* his sin.

c. **For if the truth of God has increased through my lie to His glory, why am I also still judged as a sinner?** Paul re-states the objection of an imaginary questioner: "If God will glorify Himself through my lie, how can He judge me, since I seem to indirectly increase His glory?"

d. **Let us do evil that good may come**: This was a perversion of Paul's doctrine of justification by faith, and an extension of the objection of his imaginary questioner. If you take the thinking of Paul's adversary far enough, you end up saying, "Let's sin as much as we can so God can be glorified even more." This shows us that one way to examine a teaching is to extend its meaning and consequences and see where you end up.

i. Of course, **let us do evil that good may come** was *not* Paul's teaching. He was **slanderously reported** to teach this. Still, it is possible to see how this accusation came as Paul freely preached forgiveness and salvation by grace through faith in Jesus, not works.

ii. Most Christian preaching is so far from the true gospel of free grace that Paul preached that there is no way anyone could even **slanderously** report that they taught "**let us do evil that good may come.**" If we find ourselves sometimes accused of preaching a gospel that is "too open" and too centered on faith and grace and God's work then we find ourselves in good company with Paul.

e. **Their condemnation is just**: Paul will not even *answer* such an absurd twisting of his gospel. He simply says of those who would teach such things or accuse Paul of teaching them, **their condemnation is just**. God *rightly* condemns anyone who teaches or believes such a thing.

i. Twisting the glorious free gift of God in Jesus into a *supposed* license to sin is perhaps the peak of man's depravity. It takes the most beautiful gift of God and perverts it and mocks it. This twisting is so sinful Paul saves it for last, because it is beyond the depravity of the pagan (Romans 1:24-32), beyond the hypocrisy of the moralist (Romans 2:1-5), and beyond the false confidence of the Jew (Romans 2:17-29).

B. Conclusion: the universal guilt of mankind before God.

1. (9) The guilt of both Jew and Gentile before God.

What then? Are we better *than they?* Not at all. For we have previously charged both Jews and Greeks that they are all under sin.

a. **Are we better than they? Not at all**: Since Paul was Jewish by birth and heritage (Philippians 3:4-6), when he says "**we**" he means "**we Jews.**" The point is that by nature, the Jewish person is no more right with God than the pagan or the moralist. Paul demonstrates that the pagan, the moralist, and the Jew are all **under sin** and under condemnation.

b. **Under sin**: This is a powerful phrase. It speaks of our *slavery* to sin, literally meaning "*sold* **under sin.**" By nature every person knows what it is like to be a slave to sin, **both Jews and Greeks.**

i. "Under the power of sin, but chiefly under the guilt of sin." (Poole)

ii. Morris on **under sin**: "He is regarding sin as a tyrant ruler, so that sinners are 'under' it (Jerusalem Bible, 'under sin's dominion'); they cannot break free."

2. (10-18) The Old Testament witnesses to the universal depravity and guilt of mankind.

As it is written: "There is none righteous, no, not one; there is none who understands; there is none who seeks after God. They have all turned aside; they have together become unprofitable; there is none who does good, no, not one."

"Their throat *is* an open tomb; with their tongues they have practiced deceit";

"The poison of asps *is* under their lips"; "Whose mouth *is* full of cursing and bitterness."

"Their feet *are* swift to shed blood; destruction and misery *are* in their ways; and the way of peace they have not known."

"There is no fear of God before their eyes."

> a. **There is none righteous, no, not one**: These quotations from the Psalms (Psalms 14:1-3; 5:9, 140:3, 10:7 and 36:1) and from Isaiah 59:7-8 all support this opening statement.
>
> > i. Paul looks at the human condition from top to bottom. He begins with the head and moves down to the feet. Warren Wiersbe calls this passage "An X-ray study of the lost sinner, from head to foot."
> >
> > ii. This look at the human condition is depressing. What's the point? The Apostle Paul wants us to understand our complete inability to save ourselves. The fall touches every part of man's being, and the inventory of body parts corrupted by the fall demonstrates this.
>
> b. **There is none righteous, no, not one**: When God finds none righteous, it is because there are *none*. It isn't as if there were some and God couldn't see them. There has never been a *truly* righteous man apart from Jesus Christ. "Even Adam was not righteous: he was innocent - not knowing good and evil." (Newell)
>
> c. **There is none who seeks after God**: We deceive ourselves into thinking that man, on his own, really does seek after God. But don't all the religion and rituals and practices from the beginning of time demonstrate that man seeks after God? Not at all. If man initiates the search then he doesn't seek the true God, the God of the Bible. Instead he seeks an idol that he makes himself.
>
> > i. "You have gone through this form of worship, but you have not sought after God. I am sick of this empty religiousness. We see it everywhere; it is not communion with God, it is not getting to God; indeed, God is not in it at all." (Spurgeon)

d. They have together become unprofitable: The word **unprofitable** has the idea of _rotten fruit_. It speaks of something that was permanently bad and therefore useless.

e. Their throat is an open tomb: With these references from the Psalms, Paul calls virtually every part of man's body into guilt. The **throat, tongue, lips, mouth, feet**, and **eyes** are filled with sin and rebellion against God.

> **i. Their feet are swift to shed blood**: "For further details, read your daily papers!" (Newell). For example, the _Los Angeles Times_ reported that in 1992 murders reached a record level of 800 in Los Angeles County.

f. There is no fear of God before their eyes: This summarizes the entire thought. Every sin and rebellion against God happens because we do not have a proper respect for Him. Wherever there is **sin**, there **is no fear of God**.

> **i.** John Calvin on the **fear of God**: "In short, as it is a bridle to restrain our wickedness, so when it is wanting, we feel at liberty to indulge every kind of licentiousness."

3. (19-20) Summation: the law cannot save us from our sin and the penalty it deserves.

Now we know that whatever the law says, it says to those who are under the law, that every mouth may be stopped, and all the world may become guilty before God. Therefore by the deeds of the law no flesh will be justified in His sight, for by the law _is_ the knowledge of sin.

a. Whatever the law says: Paul points out that this horrific description of man's utter sinfulness come to us **in the law**; and it is intended for **those under the law**, to silence every critic and to demonstrate the universal guilt of mankind - that **all the world may become guilty before God**.

> **i.** "We may add, that though all the vices here enumerated are not found conspicuously in every individual, yet they may be justly and truly ascribed to human nature, as we have already observed." (Calvin)

b. It says to those who are under the law: If God speaks this way to those who had the law, and attempted to _do_ the law, it is evident that **by the deeds of the law no flesh will be justified in His sight**.

> **i.** Remember that many Jewish people of Paul's day took every passage of the Old Testament describing evil and applied it only to the Gentiles - not to themselves. Paul makes it clear that God speaks **to those who are under the law**.

c. **Therefore by the deeds of the law no flesh will be justified in His sight**: The law cannot save us. The law can't justify anyone. It is useful in giving us **the knowledge of sin**, but it cannot save us.

i. Since the time of Adam and Eve, people have tried to justify themselves **by the deeds of the law**. In the Garden of Eden Adam tried to make himself presentable to God by making coverings out of fig leaves - and he failed. In Job, the oldest book of the Bible, the problem is presented clearly: *how can a man be righteous before God?* (Job 9:2). God makes part of the answer clear here through Paul - the answer is *not* in the performance of good works, in **the deeds of the law**.

ii. How we need to deeply understand this - that **by the deeds of the law no flesh will be justified!**

- This means that the law, having been broken, now can only condemn us - it can never save us
- This means that even if we could now begin to perfectly keep the law of God it could not make up for past disobedience, or remove present guilt
- This means that keeping the law is NOT God's way of salvation or of blessing under the New Covenant

d. **For by the law is the knowledge of sin**: J.B. Phillip's paraphrase of this phrase is striking. He writes, *"it is the straight-edge of the Law that shows us how crooked we are."*

i. "Lest any should think that the law hereupon is useless, he goes on to show its use, but a quite contrary one to what they intended." (Poole)

C. The revelation of the righteousness of God.

1. (21) The revelation of righteousness.

But now the righteousness of God apart from the law is revealed, being witnessed by the Law and the Prophets,

a. **But now**: These words provide the most glorious transition from the judgment of Romans 3:20 to the justification of Romans 3:21.

i. **But now** speaks of the newness of God's work in Jesus Christ - it really is a *New* Covenant. **Being witnessed by the Law and the Prophets** reminds us that there is still continuity with God's work in former times.

b. **Apart from the law**: The law cannot save us, but God reveals a **righteousness** that will save us, **apart from the law**. This is the essence of God's plan of salvation in Jesus Christ. It is a salvation that is offered **apart from the law**, apart from our own earning and deserving, apart from our own merits.

c. **Being witnessed by the Law and the Prophets**: This **righteousness** is not a novelty. Paul didn't "invent" it. It was predicted long ago, being **witnessed by the Law and the Prophets**. The Old Testament said this **righteousness** was coming.

d. **Apart from the law**: It isn't that the **righteousness of God** is revealed apart from the Old Testament, but that it is revealed apart from the *principle* of law. It is **apart** from a legal relationship to God, based on the idea of earning and deserving merit before Him.

> i. "The Greek puts to the very front this great phrase *apart from law* (*choris nomou*) and this sets forth most strongly the altogether separateness of this Divine righteousness from any law-performance, any works of man, whatsoever." (Newell)

> ii. God's righteousness is not offered to us as something to take up the slack between our ability to keep the law and God's perfect standard. It is not given to *supplement* our own righteousness, it is given completely **apart** from our own attempted righteousness.

2. (22) How this righteousness is communicated to man.

Even the righteousness of God, through faith in Jesus Christ, to all and on all who believe. For there is no difference;

a. **To all and on all who believe**: In Romans 3:21, Paul told us how this righteousness *does not* come. It *does not* come through the deeds of the law, it is *apart from the law*. Now Paul tells us how this saving righteousness *does* come. It is **through faith in Jesus Christ to all and on all who believe**.

b. **Through faith in Jesus Christ**: The righteousness of God is not ours *by* faith; it is ours **through faith**. We do not *earn* righteousness *by our faith*. We *receive* righteousness **through faith in Jesus Christ**.

> i. **Through faith** "points to the fact that faith is not a merit, earning salvation. It is no more than the means *through* which the gift is given." (Morris)

> ii. "But faith is not 'trusting' or 'expecting' God to do something, but relying on His testimony concerning the person of Christ as His Son, and the work of Christ for us on the cross . . . *After saving faith, the life of trust begins* . . . trust is always looking forward to what God will do; but faith sees that what God says has been done, and believes God's Word, having the conviction that it is true, and true for ourselves." (Newell)

c. **For the there is no difference**: There is no other way to obtain this righteousness. This righteousness is not *earned* through obedience to the law; it is a *received* righteousness, gained through faith in Jesus Christ.

i. "There is a little book entitled, *Every man his own lawyer*. Well, nowadays, according to some people, it seems as if every man is to be his own saviour; but if I had, say; a dozen gospels, and I had to sort them out, and give the right gospel to the right man, what a fix I should be in! I believe that, oftentimes, I should be giving your gospel to someone else, and someone else's gospel to you; and what a muddle it would all be! But now we have one universal cure . . . The blood and righteousness of Jesus Christ will save every man who trusts him, for 'there is no difference.' " (Spurgeon)

3. (23-24) Man's universal need and God's universal offer.

For all have sinned and fall short of the glory of God, being justified freely by His grace through the redemption that is in Christ Jesus,

a. **Being justified**: Paul develops his teaching about salvation around three themes.

- *Justification* is an image from the court of law
- *Redemption* is an image from the slave market
- *Propitiation* is an image from the world of religion, appeasing God through sacrifice

i. *Justification* solves the problem of man's *guilt* before a righteous Judge. *Redemption* solves the problem of man's *slavery* to sin, the world, and the devil. *Propitiation* solves the problem of offending our Creator.

b. **All have sinned and fall short of the glory of God**: This universal statement is answered by a universal offer to be **justified freely by His grace**. It is open to everyone who will believe.

i. Morris, quoting Moule: "The harlot, the liar, the murderer, are short of it; but so are you. Perhaps they stand at the bottom of a mine, and you on the crest of an Alp; but you are as little able to touch the stars as they." Everyone falls short, but everyone can be **justified freely by His grace**.

c. **Fall short of the glory of God**: It's impossible to describe every way we fall short, but here are four important ways man falls **short of the glory of God**.

i. We fail to give God the glory due Him, in our words, thoughts and actions.

ii. We fail to qualify for, and thereby reject the glory and reward that God gives faithful servants.

iii. We fail to properly reflect God's glory by refusing to be conformed into His image.

iv. We fail to obtain the final glory God will bestow on His people at the end of all history.

d. **Justified freely by His grace**: Being in such a sinful state, the only way we can be **justified** is to be **justified freely**. We can't purchase it without good works at all. If it isn't made free to us, we can't have it all. So we are **justified freely by His grace** - His unmerited favor, given to us without regard to what we deserve. It is a giving motivated purely by the giver, and motivated by nothing in the one who receives.

i. **Freely** is the ancient Greek word *dorean*. The way this word is used in other New Testament passages helps us understand the word. Matthew 10:8 (*Freely you have received, freely give*) and Revelation 22:17 (*And whoever desires, let him take the water of life freely*) show that the word means truly *free*, not just "cheap" or "discounted." Perhaps the most striking use of the ancient Greek word *dorean* is in John 15:25: *They hated me without a cause* (*dorean*). Even as there was *nothing* in Jesus deserving of man's hatred, so there is *nothing* in us deserving of justification - all the reasons are in God.

ii. Calvin on the use of both the words **freely** and **grace**: "He thus repeats the word to show that the whole is from God, and nothing from us . . . lest we should imagine a half kind of grace, he affirms more strongly what he means by a repetition, and claims for God's mercy alone the whole glory of our righteousness."

e. **Through the redemption that is in Christ Jesus**: Again, Paul's gospel centers squarely **in Christ Jesus**. Salvation is possible because of the **redemption** found in Him. God *cannot* give us His righteousness apart from Jesus Christ.

f. **Redemption**: This has the idea of *buying back* something, and involves *cost*. However, God pays the cost and so we are **justified freely**.

i. The word translated **redemption** had its origin describing the release of prisoners of war on payment of a price and was known as the "ransom." As time went on, it was extended to include the freeing of slaves, again by the payment of a price.

ii. The idea of **redemption** means that Jesus *bought* us; therefore, we belong to Him. Paul expressed this thought in another letter: *For you were bought at a price; therefore glorify God in your body and in your spirit, which are God's* (1 Corinthians 6:20).

4. (25-26) How the death of Jesus satisfies the righteous judgment of God.

Whom God set forth *as* a propitiation by His blood, through faith, to demonstrate His righteousness, because in His forbearance God had

passed over the sins that were previously committed, to demonstrate at the present time His righteousness, that He might be just and the justifier of the one who has faith in Jesus.

a. **Whom God set forth as a propitiation**: Jesus, by His death (**by His blood**) was a **propitiation** (substitute sacrifice) for us. As He was judged in our place, the Father could **demonstrate His righteousness** in judgment against sin, while sparing those who deserved the judgment.

> i. Wuest on **propitiation**: "The word in its classical form was used of the act of appeasing the Greek gods by a sacrifice . . . in other words, the sacrifice was offered to buy off the anger of the god."

> ii. The NIV translates **propitiation** as *sacrifice of atonement*; the Living Bible has: *to take the punishment for our sins.*

b. **A propitiation**: The ancient Greek word for **propitiation** (*hilasterion*) is also used in the Septuagint for the *mercy seat*, the lid covering the Ark of the Covenant, upon which sacrificial blood was sprinkled as an atonement for sin. While it might be said that this passage means "Jesus is our mercy seat," it probably has the more straightforward idea of **propitiation** - a substitute sacrifice.

> i. At the same time, the "mercy seat" idea should not be neglected as an illustration of propitiation. Inside the Ark of the Covenant was the evidence of man's great sin: the tablets of law; the manna received ungratefully; the budded rod of Aaron, showing man's rejection of God's leadership. Up over the Ark of the Covenant were the symbols of the holy presence of the enthroned God in the beautiful gold cherubim. In between the two stood the mercy seat, and as sacrificial blood was sprinkled on the mercy seat on the Day of Atonement (Leviticus 16), God's wrath was averted because a substitute had been slain on behalf of sinners coming by faith. We really can say that Jesus is our "mercy seat," standing between guilty sinners and the holiness of God.

c. **Whom God set forth as a propitiation**: This shows that Jesus did not somehow appease a reluctant, unwilling Father to hold back His wrath. Instead, it was God the Father who initiated the propitiation: **whom God set forth**.

d. **Passed over the sins**: God, **in His forbearance**, had **passed over** the sins of those Old Testament saints who trusted in the coming Messiah. At the cross, those sins were no longer **passed over**, they were *paid for.*

> i. The idea is that through the animal sacrifice of the Old Testament, those who looked in faith to the coming Messiah had their sins "covered" by a sort of an "IOU" or promissory note. That temporary covering was redeemed for full payment at the cross.

ii. The work of Jesus on the cross freed God from the charge that He lightly passed over sin committed before the cross. Those sins were **passed over** for a time but they were finally *paid for*.

e. **That He might be just and the justifier of the one who has faith in Jesus**: At the cross, God demonstrated His righteousness by offering man *justification* (a legal verdict of "not guilty"), while remaining completely **just** (because the righteous penalty of sin had been paid at the cross).

  i. It's easy to see how someone could be only **just** - simply send every guilty sinner to hell, as a **just** judge would do. It's easy to see how someone could only be **the justifier** - simply tell every guilty sinner, "I declare a pardon. You are all declared 'not guilty.'" But only God could find a way to be *both* **just and the justifier of the one who has faith in Jesus**.

  ii. "Here we learn that God designed to give the most *evident displays* of both his *justice* and *mercy*. Of his *justice*, in requiring a *sacrifice*, and absolutely refusing to give salvation to a lost world in any other way; and of his *mercy*, in *providing* THE sacrifice which his justice required." (Clarke)

5. (27) Boasting in the salvation which comes through the gospel of Jesus Christ is excluded.

Where *is* boasting then? It is excluded. By what law? Of works? No, but by the law of faith.

  a. **Where is boasting then?** It shouldn't be anywhere. Because we are **justified freely by His grace**, there is no room for self-congratulation or credit.

  b. **By what law?** Boasting and pride are not **excluded** because there is some specific passage in the law against them. Instead, pride is excluded because it is completely incompatible with the salvation that is freely ours though faith. Boasting is excluded **by the law of faith**.

  c. **By the law of faith**: No room for boasting! This is why the natural man *hates* being justified freely by His grace. Grace absolutely refuses to recognize his (imagined) merits and gives no place to his pride whatsoever.

6. (28-30) Justification (acquittal in the court of God) is found, for both Jew and Gentile, **apart from the deeds of the law**.

Therefore we conclude that a man is justified by faith apart from the deeds of the law. Or *is* He the God of the Jews only? *Is* He not also the God of the Gentiles? Yes, of the Gentiles also, since *there is* one God who will justify the circumcised by faith and the uncircumcised through faith.

a. **Justified by faith apart from the deeds of the law**: It isn't that we are **justified by faith** *plus* whatever **deeds of the law** we can do. We are **justified by faith** *alone*, **apart from the deeds of the law**.

i. "Since all *works of law* are barred out, *faith* alone is left. Luther so translated, and since his time *Sola Fide* has become a slogan." (Lenski)

b. **Apart from the deeds of the law**: Doesn't James contradict this in passages like James 2:14-26? How can we say that it is faith *alone* that saves, **apart from the deeds of the law?**

i. It is true faith alone saves, but true faith, saving faith, has a distinct character. It is not just agreeing with certain facts, but it is directing the mind and will in agreement with God. The whole purpose of the book of James is to describe the character of this saving faith.

ii. Calvin explains: "What James says, that man is not justified by faith alone, but also by works, does not at all militate against the preceding view [of justification by faith alone]. The reconciling of the two views depends chiefly on the drift of the argument pursued by James. For the question with him is not, how men attain righteousness before God, but how they prove it to others that they are justified; for his object was to confute hypocrites, who vainly boasted that they had faith . . . James meant no more than that man is not made or proved to be just by a feigned or dead faith, and that he must prove his righteousness by his works."

c. **Yes, of the Gentiles also**: This righteousness is offered to both **Jew** and **Gentile**. The universal character of the offer is demonstrated by a simple fact: **Is He not also the God of the Gentiles?** Of course He is. If there is only one God, then God is **God of the Gentiles** as much as He is God of the Jews. It's just up to **the Gentiles** to *recognize* Him as God.

d. **There is one God who will justify the circumcised by faith and the uncircumcised through faith**: Not only is this righteousness *available* to both Jew and Gentile, it is also *received the same way* by both Jew and Gentile. Since one God justifies both Jew and Gentile, He justifies them in the same way: **by faith . . . through faith.**

7. (31) What of the law then?

Do we then make void the law through faith? Certainly not! On the contrary, we establish the law.

a. **Do we then make void the law through faith?** We can see how someone might ask, "If the law doesn't make us righteous, what good is it? Paul, you have just made the law **void**. You are going against the law of God."

b. **Certainly not!** Of course, Paul does not **make void the law**. As the Apostle will demonstrate in Romans 4, the law *anticipated* the coming gospel of justification by faith, apart from the deeds of the law. Therefore, the gospel *establishes the law*, fulfilling its own predictions.

Romans 4 - Abraham and David Demonstrate Righteousness Apart from Works

A. Abraham is declared righteous through faith.

1. (1-3) Abraham was not justified by works, but declared righteous through faith.

What then shall we say that Abraham our father has found according to the flesh? For if Abraham was justified by works, he has *something* to boast about, but not before God. For what does the Scripture say? "Abraham believed God, and it was accounted to him for righteousness."

a. **What then shall we say**: In building on the thought begun in Romans 3:31 Paul asks the question, "Does the idea of justification through faith, apart from the works of the law, make what God did in the Old Testament irrelevant?"

b. **What then shall we say that Abraham our father has found**: In answering that question, Paul looks at Abraham, who was the most esteemed man among the Jewish people of his day - even greater than the "George Washington" of the Jewish people.

c. **For if Abraham was justified by works, he has something to boast about**: If anyone could be justified by works, they would have **something to boast about**. Nevertheless such boasting is nothing before God (**but not before God**).

i. This boasting is nothing before God because even if works *could* justify a man, he would in some way still *fall short of the glory of God* (Romans 3:23).

ii. This boasting is nothing because **before God**, every pretense is stripped away and it is evident that no one can really be **justified by works**.

d. **For what does the Scripture say?** The Old Testament does not say Abraham was declared righteous because of his works. Instead, Genesis 15:6 says that **Abraham believed God and it was accounted to him for righteousness**.

i. Paul makes it clear: Abraham's righteousness did not come from performing good works, but from belief in God. It was a righteousness obtained through faith.

ii. Generally, the Jewish teachers of Paul's day believed that Abraham was justified by his works, by keeping the law. Ancient passages from the rabbis say: "We find that Abraham our father had performed the whole Law before it was given" and "Abraham was perfect in all his deeds with the Lord." The rabbis argued that Abraham kept the law perfectly before it was given, keeping it by intuition or anticipation.

iii. The Apostle Paul does not say that Abraham was *made* righteous in all of his doings, but God **accounted** Abraham as righteous. Our justification is not God *making* us perfectly righteous, but *counting* us as perfectly righteous. After we are *counted* righteous, then God begins making us truly righteous, culminating at our resurrection.

iv. "*Counted* is *logizomai*. It was used in early secular documents; 'put down to one's account, let my revenues be placed on deposit at the storehouse; I now give orders generally with regard to all payments actually made or credited to the government.' Thus, God put to Abraham's account, placed on deposit for him, credited to him, righteousness . . . Abraham possessed righteousness in the same manner as a person would possess a sum of money placed in his account in a bank." (Wuest)

v. Genesis 15:6 does not tell us how other men *accounted* Abraham. Instead, it tells us how God **accounted** him. "Moses [in Genesis] does not, indeed, tell us what men thought of him [Abraham], but how he was accounted before the tribunal of God." (Calvin)

vi. Remember that **righteousness** is also more than the *absence* of evil and guilt. It is a *positive* good, meaning that God does not only declare us *innocent*, but *righteous*.

2. (4-5) A distinction made between grace and works.

Now to him who works, the wages are not counted as grace but as debt. But to him who does not work but believes on Him who justifies the ungodly, his faith is accounted for righteousness,

a. **Now to him who works, the wages are not counted as grace**: The idea of **grace** stands opposite to the principle of **works**; grace has to do with *receiving* the freely given gift of God, works has to do with *earning* our merit before God.

    i. Wuest on *charis*, the ancient Greek word translated **grace**: "Signified in classical authors a favor done out of the spontaneous generosity of the heart without any expectation or return. Of course, this favor was always done to one's friend, never to an enemy . . . But when *charis* comes into the New Testament, it takes an infinite leap forward, for the favor God did at Calvary was for those who hated Him."

b. **Not counted as grace but as debt**: A system of works seeks to put God in **debt** to us, making God *owe* us His favor because of our good behavior. In works-thinking, God *owes* us salvation or blessing because of our good works.

    i. God isn't praising laziness here. "The antithesis is not simply between the worker and the non-worker but between the worker and person who does not work *but believes*." (Murray)

c. **But to him who does not work but believes on Him who justifies the ungodly, his faith is accounted for righteousness**: Righteousness can never be accounted to the one who approaches God on the principle of works. Instead it is given to the one **who believes on Him who justifies the ungodly**.

d. **Him who justifies the ungodly**: This is who God justifies - **the ungodly**. We might expect God would only justify a godly man but because of what Jesus did on the cross, God can justify **the ungodly**.

    i. It isn't as if God is *happy* with our **ungodly** condition. We are not justified *because* of our ungodliness, but *despite* our ungodliness.

    ii. Morris quoting Denney: "The paradoxical phrase, *Him that justifieth the ungodly*, does not suggest that justification is a fiction, whether legal or of any other sort, but that it is a miracle."

e. **Faith is accounted for righteousness**: Just as Abraham, so our **faith is accounted for righteousness**. This was not some special arrangement for Abraham alone. We can enter into this relationship with God also.

    i. By this we understand that there are not two ways of salvation - saved by works through law-keeping in the Old Testament and saved by grace through faith in the New Testament. Everyone who has ever been saved - Old or New Testament - is saved by grace through faith, through their relationship of a trusting love with God. Because of the New Covenant we have *benefits* of salvation that Old Testament saints did not have but we do not have a different *manner* of salvation.

©3. (6-8) David and the blessedness of justification through faith.

Just as David also describes the blessedness of the man to whom God imputes righteousness apart from works: "Blessed *are those* whose lawless deeds are forgiven, and whose sins are covered; blessed *is the* man to whom the LORD shall not impute sin."

a. **Just as David also describes**: King David of the Old Testament knew what it was like to be a guilty sinner. He knew the seriousness of sin and how good it is to be truly forgiven. He knew **the blessedness of the man to whom God imputes righteousness apart from works**. If David were judged on works alone, the righteous God must condemn him; nevertheless he knew by experience that **blessed are those whose lawless deeds are forgiven**.

i. "No sinner, and try he ever so hard, can possibly carry his own sins away and come back cleansed of guilt. No amount of money, no science, no inventive skill, no armies of millions, nor any other earthly power can carry away from the sinner one little sin and its guilt. Once it is committed, every sin and its guilt cling to the sinner as close as does his own shadow, cling to all eternity unless God carries them away." (Lenski)

b. **To whom God imputes righteousness apart from works . . . blessed is the man to whom the LORD shall not impute sin**: David agrees with Abraham regarding the idea of an *imputed* righteousness, a goodness that is *given*, not earned.

i. "Our adversaries the papists oppose the imputation of Christ's righteousness to us; they cavil at the very word . . . and yet the apostle useth the word ten times in this chapter." (Poole)

c. **Blessed is the man**: In the Psalm quoted (Psalm 32:1-2), David speaks of the blessedness, *not* of the one who is justified through works, but of the one who is cleansed through *imputation*. This is centered on what God places upon us (the righteousness of Jesus), not on what we do for God.

4. (9-12) Abraham was counted righteous before he was circumcised; therefore he was not counted righteous *because* he was circumcised.

Does this blessedness then *come* upon the circumcised *only*, or upon the uncircumcised also? For we say that faith was accounted to Abraham for righteousness. How then was it accounted? While he was circumcised, or uncircumcised? Not while circumcised, but while uncircumcised. And he received the sign of circumcision, a seal of the righteousness of the faith which *he had while still* uncircumcised, that he might be the father of all those who believe, though they are uncircumcised, that righteousness might be imputed to them also, and the father of

circumcision to those who not only *are* of the circumcision, but who also walk in the steps of the faith which our father Abraham *had while still* uncircumcised.

a. **Does this blessedness then come upon the circumcised only, or upon the uncircumcised also?** If we are counted righteous by God because of **faith**, not because of **circumcision** (or any other ritual), then the **blessedness** mentioned in Romans 4:7 can be given to the **uncircumcised** Gentiles by faith.

b. **How then was it accounted? While he was circumcised, or uncircumcised?** Abraham was counted as righteous in Genesis 15:6. He did not receive the covenant of circumcision until Genesis 17, which was at least 14 years later. Therefore his righteousness wasn't based on circumcision, but on **faith**.

c. **The faith which he had while still uncircumcised**: In fact, Abraham, **the father of all those who believe**, was declared righteous while he was still *uncircumcised*! Therefore, how could anyone then say (as some did in Paul's day) that Gentiles must be circumcised before God would declare them righteous?

   i. For the Jewish people of Paul's day, the significance of circumcision was more than social. It was the entry point for a life lived under the Law of Moses: *And I testify again to every man who becomes circumcised that he is a debtor to keep the whole law* (Galatians 5:3).

d. **That he might be the father of all those who believe, though they are uncircumcised . . . who also walk in the steps of the faith which our father Abraham had while still uncircumcised**: The Jews of Paul's day thought circumcision meant they were the true descendents of Abraham. Paul insists that to have Abraham as your father, you must **walk in the steps of the faith** that Abraham walked in.

   i. "**Our father Abraham**" is an important phrase, one that the ancient Jews jealously guarded. They did not allow a circumcised Gentile convert to Judaism refer to Abraham as "our father" in the synagogue. A Gentile convert had to call Abraham "your father" and only natural born Jews could call Abraham "our father." Paul throws out that distinction, and says that through faith, all can say, "**our father Abraham.**"

   ii. It must have been a shock for the Jewish readers of this letter to see that Paul called Abraham the father of **uncircumcised** people! **Faith**, not circumcision, is the vital link to Abraham. It is far more important to have Abraham's faith (and the righteousness imputed to him because of it) than it is to have Abraham's circumcision.

iii. William Barclay explains that the Jewish teachers of Paul's day had a saying: "What is written of Abraham is also written of his children," meaning that promises given to Abraham extend to his descendants. Paul heartily agreed with this principle, and extended the principle of being justified by faith to all Abraham's *spiritual* descendants, those who believe, **who also walk in the steps of the faith** of Abraham.

5. (13-15) God's promise to Abraham was based on the principle of faith, not law or works.

For the promise that he would be the heir of the world *was* not to Abraham or to his seed through the law, but through the righteousness of faith. For if those who are of the law *are* heirs, faith is made void and the promise made of no effect, because the law brings about wrath; for where there is no law *there is* no transgression.

a. **For the promise that he would be the heir of the world was not to Abraham or to his seed through the law**: Since all God's dealings with Abraham, Isaac, and Jacob happened before the giving of the Mosaic Law, we can't say they were based on the law. Instead, they are based on God's declaration of Abraham's righteousness through faith.

i. "Faith is the ground of God's blessing. Abraham was a blessed man, indeed, but he became *heir of the world* on another principle entirely - simple faith." (Newell)

b. **For the promise . . . through the righteousness of faith**: The law cannot bring us into the blessings of God's promises. This is not because the law is bad, but because we are unable to keep it.

c. **Because the law brings about wrath**: Our inability to keep the law (our **transgression**) means that it becomes essentially a vehicle of God's wrath towards us, especially if we regard it as the principle by which we are justified and relate to God.

d. **Where there is no law there is no transgression**: How can Paul say this? Because "*Transgression* is the right word for overstepping a line, and this for breaking a clearly defined commandment" (Morris). Where there is no line, there is no actual **transgression**.

i. There is sin that is not the "crossing the line" of the Law of Moses. The root of sin isn't in breaking the law, but in breaking *trust* with God; with denying His loving, caring purpose in every command He gives. Before Adam sinned he broke *trust* with God - therefore God's plan of redemption is centered on a relationship of trusting love - *faith* - instead of law-keeping. When we center our relationship with God on law-keeping instead of trusting love, we go against His whole plan.

B. Following Abraham's example.

1. (16) Justification according to grace, through faith.

Therefore *it is* of faith that *it might be* according to grace, so that the promise might be sure to all the seed, not only to those who are of the law, but also to those who are of the faith of Abraham, who is the father of us all

> a. **It is of faith that it might be according to grace**: **Faith** is related to **grace** in the same way *works* is related to *law*. Grace and law are principles, and faith and works are the means by which we pursue those principles for our relationship with God.
>
> > i. To speak technically, we are not saved by *faith*. We are saved by God's *grace*, and *grace* is appropriated by *faith*.
>
> b. **It is of faith**: Salvation is **of faith** and nothing else. We can only receive salvation by the principle of **grace** through **faith**. **Grace** can't be gained through **works**, whether they be past works, present works, or promised works. This is because by definition **grace** is given without regard to anything in the one who receives it.
>
> > i. "Grace and faith are congruous, and will draw together in the same chariot, but grace and merit are contrary the one to the other and pull opposite ways, and therefore God has not chosen to yoke them together." (Spurgeon)
>
> c. **So that the promise might be sure to all the seed**: The **promise** can only be **sure** if it is according to **grace**. If law is the basis of our salvation, then our salvation depends on our performance in keeping the law - and no one can keep the law good enough to be saved by it. A law-promise of salvation can never be **sure**.
>
> > i. If the promise "were of the law, it would be unsure and uncertain, because of man's weakness, who is not able to perform it." (Poole)
>
> d. **But also to those who are of the faith of Abraham, who is the father of us all**: If our relationship with God is **according to grace** (not circumcision or law-keeping), then that relationship is for **those who are of the faith of Abraham**, even if they are not of his lineage.
>
> > i. A Gentile could say, "I am not a Jew, I am not of the law; but I am of the **faith of Abraham**," and he would be just as saved as a Jewish believer in Jesus would be.
>
> e. **The father of us all**: The fulfillment of the promise in Genesis 17:4-5 is found not only in Abraham's descendants through Isaac, but especially in his role as being **the father of us all** who believe - and those believers come from every nation under heaven.

2. (17-18) The life-giving power of the God Abraham believed in.

(As it is written, "I have made you a father of many nations") in the presence of Him whom he believed; God, who gives life to the dead and calls those things which do not exist as though they did; who, contrary to hope, in hope believed, so that he became the father of many nations, according to what was spoken, "So shall your descendants be."

a. **So that he became the father of many nations**: Even as it took a supernatural life-giving work to make Abraham the physical **father of many nations**, it also took a supernatural life-giving work to make him the spiritual **father of many nations**.

b. **Who gives life to the dead and calls those things which do not exist as if they did**: These works of God demonstrate His ability to count things that are not (such as our righteousness) as if they were (as in counting us righteous).

> i. If God could call the dead womb of Sarah to life, he can call those who are *dead in trespasses and sins* (Ephesians 2:1) to new life in Jesus.

> ii. "I'm greatly comforted when God speaks about me as righteous, justified, glorified, holy, pure, and saintly. God can talk about such things before they exist, because He knows they will exist." (Smith)

c. **Contrary to hope, in hope believed**: This life-giving power was accomplished in Abraham as he believed. The power was evident naturally and spiritually.

> i. Abraham's example also helps us to understand the nature of faith. The conception of Abraham's son Isaac was a miracle, but it was not an immaculate conception. Abraham's faith did not mean that he did nothing and just waited for God to create a child in Sarah's womb. Abraham and Sarah had marital relations and trusted God for a miraculous result. This shows us that faith does not mean doing *nothing*, but doing *everything* with trust and reliance on God.

> ii. "All true believers, like Abraham, obey. Obedience is faith in action. You are to walk in the steps of the faith of father Abraham. His faith did not sit still, it took steps; and you must take these steps also by obeying God because you believe him. That faith which has no works with it is a dead faith, and will justify no one." (Spurgeon)

> iii. "Sense corrects imagination, reason corrects sense, but faith corrects both. It will not be, saith sense; it cannot be, saith reason; it both can and will be, saith faith, for I have a promise for it." (Trapp)

3. (19-22) The character of Abraham's faith.

And not being weak in faith, he did not consider his own body, already dead (since he was about a hundred years old), and the deadness of Sarah's womb. He did not waver at the promise of God through unbelief, but was strengthened in faith, giving glory to God, and being fully convinced that what He had promised He was also able to perform. And therefore "it was accounted to him for righteousness."

a. **Not being weak in faith**: Abraham's faith was strong but it was also **strengthened**. He was **strengthened in faith**.

i. The idea seems to be that Abraham was **strengthened in** his **faith**; but Paul could also mean that Abraham was **strengthened** *by* his **faith** - certainly both were true.

ii. How we need to be **strengthened in faith**! "Dear brother, little faith will save thee if it be true faith, but there are many reasons why you should seek an increase of it." (Spurgeon)

iii. Spurgeon knew that ministers and preachers especially needed to be **strengthened in faith**. He sometimes shared his own struggles in this area from the pulpit, but wanted to make it clear that his struggles in faith should never be indulged: "Whenever, dear hearers, you catch any of us who are teachers doubting and fearing, do not pity us, but scold us. We have no right to be in Doubting Castle. Pray do not visit us there. Follow us as far as we follow Christ, but if we get into the horrible Slough of Despond, come and pull us out by the hair of our heads if necessary, but do not fall into it yourselves." (Spurgeon)

iv. "I do not think we shall have many conversions unless we expect God to bless the word, and feel certain that he will do so. We must not wonder and be astonished if we hear of a dozen or two conversions, but let the astonishment be that thousands are not converted when they hear such divine truth, and when we ask the Holy Spirit to attend it with divine energy. God will bless us in proportion to our faith. It is the rule of his kingdom - 'According to your faith so be it unto you.' O God, give thy ministers more faith! Let us believe thee firmly!" (Spurgeon)

b. **He did not consider his own body, already dead**: Abraham, in faith, did not look to circumstances (**his own body and the deadness of Sarah's womb**) but he looked **at the promise of God**.

i. In Romans 4:19, there is textual uncertainty as to if we should read *he considered his body as good as dead* or if we should read **he did not consider his own body**. Either is possible, though the second seems to be a better choice.

c. **He did not waver at the promise of God through unbelief:** His faith did not **waver**; and it **gave glory to God**. Though it was a huge challenge, Abraham remained steadfast in faith.

> i. "When there is no contest, it is true, no one, as I have said, denies that God can do all things; but as soon as anything comes in the way to impede the course of God's promise, we cast down God's power from its eminence." (Calvin)

d. **Being fully convinced that what He had promised He was also able to perform:** Abraham's faith came because he had been **fully convinced** of God's ability to perform what He has promised.

> i. Is your God too small? The God of Abraham was able to perform what He had promised, and Abraham was **fully convinced** of this.

> ii. Some people don't come to Jesus or don't go further with Him because they are not **fully convinced that what He had promised He was also able to perform.** They think, "It is fine for them but it won't work for me." This thinking is a devilish attack on faith, and must be rejected.

e. **Able to perform:** This kind of faith sees the work of God done. It sees the work of God done in the *immediate* (Isaac was born in fulfillment of the promise) and in the *eternal* (**accounted to him for righteousness**).

4. (23-25) Abraham's justification and our own.

Now it was not written for his sake alone that it was imputed to him, but also for us. It shall be imputed to us who believe in Him who raised up Jesus our Lord from the dead, who was delivered up because of our offenses, and was raised because of our justification.

a. **It was not written for his sake alone:** It wasn't only for Abraham's benefit that God declared him righteous through faith; he is an example that we are invited to follow - it is **also for us**. Paul's confidence is glorious: **It shall be imputed to us who believe**; this wasn't just for Abraham, but for us also.

b. **Who believe in Him who raised up Jesus:** When we talk about faith and saving faith in Jesus, it is important to emphasize that we mean believing that His work on the cross (**delivered up because of our offenses**) and triumph over sin and death (**raised because of our justification**) is what saves us. There are many false-faiths that can never save, and only faith in what Jesus accomplished on the cross and through the empty tomb can save us.

- Faith in the historical events of the life of Jesus will not save
- Faith in the beauty of Jesus' life will not save

- Faith in the accuracy or goodness of Jesus' teaching will not save
- Faith in the deity of Jesus and in His Lordship will not save
- *Only* faith in what the real Jesus did for us on the cross will save

c. **Raised because of our justification**: The resurrection has an essential place in our redemption because it demonstrates God the Father's perfect satisfaction with the Son's work on the cross. It proves that what Jesus did on the cross was in fact a perfect sacrifice made by One who remained perfect, even though bearing the sin of the world.

i. **Delivered up because of our offenses**: The ancient Greek word translated **delivered** (*paradidomi*) was used of casting people into prison or delivering them to justice. "Here it speaks of the judicial act of God the Father delivering God the Son to the justice that required the payment of the penalty for human sin." (Wuest)

ii. "Jesus' resurrection always includes his sacrificial death but it brings out the all-sufficiency of his death. If death had held him, he would have failed; since he was raised from death, his sacrifice sufficed, God set his seal upon it by raising him up." (Lenski)

iii. "Christ did meritoriously work our justification and salvation by his death and passion, but the efficacy and perfection thereof with respect to us depend on his resurrection . . . This one verse is an abridgement of the whole gospel." (Poole)

iv. In this chapter, Paul clearly demonstrated that in no way does the Old Testament contradict the gospel of salvation by grace through faith.   Instead the gospel is the *fulfillment* of the Old Testament, and Abraham - justified through faith - is our pattern.

Romans 5 - Benefits of Being Justified through Faith

"In the whole Bible there is hardly another chapter which can equal this triumphant text." (Martin Luther)

A. The benefits of believing.

1. (1-2) Peace and a standing of grace.

Therefore, having been justified by faith, we have peace with God through our Lord Jesus Christ, through whom also we have access by faith into this grace in which we stand, and rejoice in hope of the glory of God.

a. **Therefore, having been justified by faith**: To this point in the Book of Romans, Paul has convinced us all that the only way of salvation is to be justified by grace through faith. Now he will tell us what the practical benefits of this are, explaining that it is more than an interesting idea.

i. **Justified by faith** speaks of a *legal decree*. Romans 1:18-3:20 found us guilty before the court of God's law, God's glory, and our conscience. Then Paul explained how because of what Jesus did, the righteousness of God is given to all who believe. The guilty sentence is transformed into a sentence of **justified**, and **justified by faith**.

b. **Peace with God through our Lord Jesus Christ**: This is the first benefit. Because the price is paid in full by the work of Jesus on the cross, God's justice towards us is eternally satisfied.

i. This is not the *peace of God* spoken of in other places (such as Philippians 4:7). This is peace **with** God; the battle between God and our self is *finished* - and He won, winning us. Some never knew they were *out of peace* with God, but they were like drivers ignoring the red lights of a police car in their rear-view mirror - they are in trouble even if they don't know it, and it will soon catch up to them.

ii. This peace can only come **through our Lord Jesus Christ**. He and His work is our entire ground for peace. In fact, Jesus *is* our peace (Ephesians 2:14).

iii. Remember that the Bible doesn't say we have peace with the devil, peace with the world, peace with the flesh, or peace with sin. Life is still a battle for the Christian but it is no longer a battle against God - it is fighting *for* Him. Some Christians are tempted to believe the battle against God was almost a better place to be, and that is a dangerous and damnable lie.

iv. "I am delighted to find that sin stings you, and that you hate it. The more hatred of sin the better. A sin-hating soul is a God-loving soul. If sin never distresses you, then God has never favored you." (Charles Spurgeon)

c. **Into this grace in which we stand**: This is the second benefit - we have a *standing* in **grace** - in God's unmerited favor. This **grace** is given *through* Jesus and gained *by* faith.

i. **Grace** (God's undeserved favor towards us) is not only the *way* salvation comes to us, it is also a description of our present standing before God. It is not only the *beginning* principle of the Christian life, it is also the *continuing* principle of the Christian life. "*We stand* translates a perfect tense, used in this sense of the present, and with the thought of a continuing attitude." (Morris)

ii. Many Christians begin in grace, but then think they must go on to perfection and maturity by dealing with God on the principle of law - on the ideas of earning and deserving. Paul spoke against this very point in Galatians 3:2-3 and Galatians 5:1-4.

iii. A standing in grace reassures us: God's present attitude towards the believer in Christ Jesus is one of favor, seeing them in terms of joy, beauty, and pleasure. He doesn't just love us; He *likes* us because we are in Jesus.

iv. Standing in grace means that:

- I don't have to prove I am worthy of God's love
- God is my friend
- The door of access is permanently open to Him
- I am free from the "score sheet" - the account is settled in Jesus
- I spend more time praising God and less time hating myself

v. "The former rebels are not merely forgiven by having their due punishment remitted; they are brought into a place of high favour with God - *this grace in which we stand*." (Bruce)

vi. *The Proper Attitude of Man under Grace* (William Newell)

- To *believe*, and consent to be *loved while unworthy*, is the great secret
- To refuse to make "resolutions" and "vows"; for that is to trust in the flesh
- To expect to be blessed, though realizing more and more lack of worth
- To testify of God's goodness, at all times
- To be certain of God's future favor; yet to be ever more tender in conscience toward Him
- To rely on God's chastening hand as a mark of His kindness
- A man under grace, if like Paul, has no burdens regarding himself; but many about others

d. **Through whom also we have access by faith**: Our **access** into this standing of grace is only by faith, and through Jesus; we cannot *work* ourselves into this standing. The **access** isn't just into a standing of grace, but into the very courts of heaven. This is a blessing beyond **peace with God**. "One may be reconciled to his prince, and yet not to be brought into his presence." (Poole)

i. Leon Morris on **access**: "The idea is that of introduction to the presence-chamber of a monarch. The rendering *access* is inadequate, as it leaves out of sight the fact that we do not come in our own strength, but need an 'introducer' - Christ."

ii. Wuest quotes Thayer regarding **access**: "That friendly relation with God whereby we are acceptable to Him and have assurance that He is favorably disposed towards us."

e. **We have access**: The perfect verb tense of **have access** also indicates that this is a standing, permanent possession. Because our standing is based on grace, we really can **stand** and have **peace**, because we know that our access is a permanent possession. It cannot be taken away at a later time.

i. "And this access to God, or *introduction* to the Divine presence, is to be considered a lasting privilege. We are not brought to God for the purpose of an *interview*, but to *remain* with him; to be his *household*; and by *faith*, to behold his face, and walk in the light of his countenance." (Clarke)

f. **Rejoice in hope of the glory of God**: This is the logical conclusion to such peace and such a standing of grace. When we relate to God on the principle of works, any rejoicing is presumptuous and any imagined glory goes to us, not God.

i. **Rejoice** is the word normally translated *boast*. It means "a triumphant, rejoicing confidence." (Morris)

ii. **Hope** never implied uncertainty for Paul. J.B. Philipps translates **hope** as *happy certainty*.

g. **Justified by faith**: Again, all this only makes sense **having been justified by faith**. If we are not justified by grace through faith, then we have no peace with God, and we have no present standing of grace.

i. "Alas, how few believers have the courage of faith! When some saint here or there does begin to believe the facts and walk in shouting liberty, we say (perhaps secretly), 'He must be an especially holy, consecrated man.' No, he is just a poor sinner like you, who is *believing* in the *abundance* of *grace*!" (Newell)

2. (3-4) The promise of glory is also for the present time.

And not only *that*, but we also glory in tribulations, knowing that tribulation produces perseverance; and perseverance, character; and character, hope.

a. **And not only that, but we also glory in tribulations**: Paul anticipates the accusation that he is too "pie in the sky," that glory for the Christian applies only to the sweet bye-and-bye. Paul replies, "I know we have many **tribulations** now but we **glory** in those also."

i. Paul isn't spinning out spiritual platitudes. First, he uses strong words. **Tribulations** is "a strong term. It does not refer to minor inconveniences, but to real hardships" (Morris). Second, Paul *lived a life full of tribulation*. Paul knew the truth of this better than most anyone.

b. **Knowing that tribulation produces perseverance**: We can **glory in tribulations** (literally, *stresses*) because they are the occasion to produce **perseverance** (endurance).

i. A runner must be stressed to gain endurance. Sailors must go to sea. Soldiers go to battle. For the Christian, tribulation is just part of our Christian life. We should not desire or hope for a tribulation-free Christian life, especially because:

- God uses tribulation wonderfully in our life
- God knows how much tribulation we can take, and He carefully measures the tribulation we face
- Those who are not Christians face tribulation also

ii. "A Christian man should be willing to be tried; he should be pleased to let his religion be put to the test. 'There,' says he, 'hammer away if you like.' Do you want to be carried to heaven on a feather bed?" (Spurgeon)

iii. "I've heard people advise others against praying for patience because God will then send them tribulations. If that's the way patience comes then, 'God, bring on the troubles.' I need patience!" (Smith)

iv. "Whatever virtues tribulation finds us in, it develops more fully. If anyone is carnal, weak, blind, wicked, irascible, haughty, and so forth, tribulation will make him more carnal, weak, blind, wicked and irritable. On the other hand, if one is spiritual, strong, wise, pious, gentle and humble, he will become more spiritual, powerful, wise, pious, gentle and humble." (Martin Luther)

v. " 'Tribulation worketh patience,' says the apostle. Naturally it is not so. Tribulation worketh impatience, and impatience misses the fruit of experience, and sours into hopelessness. Ask many who have buried a dear child, or have lost their wealth, or have suffered pain of body, and they will tell you that the natural result of affliction is to produce irritation against providence, rebellion against God, questioning, unbelief, petulance, and! all sorts of evils. But what a wonderful alteration takes place when the heart is renewed by the Holy Spirit!" (Spurgeon)

c. **Perseverance, character; and character, hope**: This is a golden chain of Christian growth and maturity. One virtue builds upon another as we grow in the pattern of Jesus.

i. Most every Christian wants to develop **character** and have more **hope**. These qualities spring out of **perseverance**, which comes through **tribulation**. We may wish to have better **character** and more **hope** without starting with **tribulation**, but that isn't God's pattern and plan.

ii. I would rather have God just sprinkle **perseverance** and **character** and **hope** on me as I sleep. I could wake up a much better Christian! But that isn't God's plan for me or for any Christian.

iii. Therefore we say - soberly, reverently - we say about tribulation, "Lord, bring it on. I know you love me and carefully measure every trial and have a loving purpose to accomplish in every tribulation. Lord, I won't seek trials and search out tribulation, but I won't despise them or lose hope when they come. I trust Your love in everything You allow."

3. (5) Evidence for hope: God's love in our hearts right now, evidenced by the presence of the Holy Spirit in our lives.

Now hope does not disappoint, because the love of God has been poured out in our hearts by the Holy Spirit who was given to us.

a. **Now hope does not disappoint**: The hope that tribulation builds in us is not a hope that will be disappointed. We are assured of this because God has proved His intention to complete His work in us - the proof being **the love of God . . . poured out in our hearts by the Holy Spirit who was given to us.**

b. **The love of God . . . poured out in our hearts**: Every Christian should have some experience of this, to have a deep inner awareness of God's love for us.

i. The Apostle Paul's logical arguments in Romans are devastating but the Book of Romans doesn't lack emotion or passionate experiences with God. Paul wants us to think the right thoughts about God, but he also wants us to have the right experience with God - **the love of God . . . poured out in our hearts**.

ii. God's love isn't given to us in a trickle, it is **poured out in our hearts**. Some Christians live as if it was only a trickle but God wants us to know the *outpouring* of His love.

c. **The Holy Spirit who was given to us**: This is how God's love is communicated - through the Holy Spirit. A lack of awareness of God's love can often be credited to a failure to be constantly filled with the Holy Spirit and to walk in the Spirit.

i. "The love of God is like light to a blind eye until the Holy Ghost opens that eye . . . may the Holy Spirit now be here in each one of us, to shed abroad the love of God in our hearts." (Spurgeon)

ii. Everyone who is a Christian *has* the Holy Spirit (Romans 8:9). But not every Christian lives in the fullness of the Holy Spirit (Ephesians 5:18), and not every Christian walks in the Spirit (Romans 8:4-5).

4. (6-8) A description of God's love towards us.

For when we were still without strength, in due time Christ died for the ungodly. For scarcely for a righteous man will one die; yet perhaps for a good man someone would even dare to die. But God demonstrates His own love toward us, in that while we were still sinners, Christ died for us.

a. **When we were still without strength**: Paul describes the greatness of God's love. It is love given to the undeserving, to those **without strength**, to the **ungodly**, to **sinners**. This emphasizes the fact that the reasons for God's love are found *in Him*, not in us.

i. Who are these people? Who are the ungodly and wicked people Jesus died for? Paul spent the first two-and-a-half chapters of the Book of Romans telling us that we *all* are those people.

b. **In due time Christ died for the ungodly**: God sent the Son at the right time, at the **due time**. It may have seemed late to some but Jesus' work was done at the perfect time in God's plan: *when the fullness of the time had come, God sent forth His Son* (Galatians 4:4).

i. The world was prepared spiritually, economically, linguistically, politically, philosophically and geographically for the coming of Jesus and the spread of the Gospel.

ii. **In due time** also has the meaning that Jesus died at the due time *for us*. He died when we were sinners who needed a Savior. His timing was just right for us.

c. **Christ died for the ungodly**: Paul mentioned the idea of a substitutionary sacrifice with the word *propitiation* in Romans 3:25. Here, he makes the point again by saying that **Christ died for the ungodly**. The ancient Greek word **for** is the word *huper*, which means "for the sake of, in behalf of, instead of."

i. Other places where *huper* is used in the New Testament help us to understand this. In John 11:50, we read: *nor do you consider that it is expedient for us that one man should die for* [huper] *the people*. Galatians 3:13 says, *Christ redeemed us from the curse of the law, having become a curse for* [huper] *us*.

ii. Therefore to genuinely say, "Jesus died for me" you must also say, "I have no strength to save myself. I am ungodly. I am a sinner." Jesus died to save and transform *these*.

iii. "You will say, 'Oh, I am one of the worst in the world.' Christ died for the worst in the world. 'Oh, but I have no power to be better.' Christ died for those that were without strength. 'Oh, but my case condemns itself.' Christ died for those that legally are condemned. 'Ay, but my case is hopeless.' Christ died for the hopeless. He is the hope of the hopeless. He is the Savior not of those partly lost, but of the wholly lost." (Spurgeon)

iv. "If Christ died for the ungodly, *this fact leaves the ungodly no excuse if they do not come to hi*m, and believe in him unto salvation. Had it been otherwise they might have pleaded, 'We are not fit to come.' But you are ungodly, and Christ died for the ungodly, why not for you?" (Spurgeon)

d. **For scarcely for a righteous man will one die**: God's love is a love beyond even the best love among humans. A good man might die a noble martyrdom for the "right kind" of person - such as a **righteous man** or a **good man**. But Jesus died for those who were neither righteous nor good.

i. Is there a difference between **a righteous man** and **a good man** in Paul's thinking? The difference in Romans 5:7 seems to be that the **righteous man** is only that - righteous in his personal life but perhaps lacking in feeling for others. The **good man** by contrast goes beyond the other man by also being kind and benevolent.

e. **But God demonstrates His own love**: How does the death of the Son demonstrate the love of the Father? Because it was harder for the Father to send His only Son, and because *God* [the Father] *was in Christ, reconciling the world to Himself* (2 Corinthians 5:19).

i. "It would be easy to see the cross as demonstrating the indifference of God, a God who let the innocent Jesus be taken by wicked men, tortured, and crucified while he did nothing . . . Unless there is a sense in which the Father and Christ are one, it is not the love of God that the cross shows." (Morris)

ii. The work of Jesus on the cross for us is God's ultimate proof of His love for you. He may give additional proof, but He can give no greater proof. If the cross is the ultimate demonstration of God's love, it is also the ultimate demonstration of man's hatred. It also proves that the height of man's hatred can't defeat the height of God's love.

iii. The *demonstration* of God's love isn't displayed so much in that Jesus died, but it is seen in whom Jesus died *for* - undeserving sinners and rebels against Him.

5. (9-11) Salvation from God's wrath.

Much more then, having now been justified by His blood, we shall be saved from wrath through Him. For if when we were enemies we were reconciled to God through the death of His Son, much more, having been reconciled, we shall be saved by His life. And not only *that*, but we also rejoice in God through our Lord Jesus Christ, through whom we have now received the reconciliation.

a. **Much more then, having now been justified by His blood, we shall be saved from wrath**: If we are justified by the work of Jesus, we can be assured that we are also **saved from wrath through Him**. The wrath of God that was *revealed from heaven against all ungodliness and unrighteousness of men* (Romans 1:18) was placed on Jesus as a substitute in the place of the believer.

i. By nature, some are inclined to preface these great promises of God with "*much less then*" regarding themselves. God wants them to see it plain and clear: **Much more then** is the love and goodness of God given to us and **much more then** can we have confidence in Him.

ii. **Saved from wrath**: Whose wrath? God's righteous wrath. It is true that we must be saved from the world, the flesh, and the devil but most of all we must be rescued from the righteous wrath of God.

iii. John Trapp on **much more then**: "It is a greater work of God to bring men to grace, than, being in the state of grace, to bring them to glory; because sin is far more distant from grace than grace is from glory."

b. **For if when we were enemies we were reconciled to God**: If God showed such dramatic love to us when **we were enemies**, think of the blessings we will enjoy once we are reconciled to God! If God does this much for His enemies, how much more will He do for His friends!

i. Wuest, quoting Alford: "Not only has the reconciled man confidence that he shall escape God's wrath, but triumphant confidence - joyful hope in God."

c. **Much more, having been reconciled, we shall be saved by His life**: This *reconciliation* isn't only helpful when we die; it also touches our life *right now*. God is forever done dealing with believers on the basis of **wrath**. He may chasten them as a loving Father, but not in punishment or payment for their sins. God only allows chastening to bring loving correction and guidance.

d. **Saved from wrath through Him . . . we were reconciled to God through the death of His Son . . . rejoice in God through our Lord Jesus . . . through whom we have now received the reconciliation**: The point is clearly emphasized. What matters is what we have **through** Jesus. What we have through our own works doesn't matter and can't help us. It's all **through** Jesus.

B. The Two Men.

1. (12) The spread of sin throughout the human race.

Therefore, just as through one man sin entered the world, and death through sin, and thus death spread to all men, because all sinned;

a. **Just as through one man sin entered the world**: The Apostle Paul regarded Genesis 3 as totally, historically true. According to Paul (and according to Jesus, as He says in Matthew 19:4-6), Adam and Eve were real people and what they did has a lasting effect to the present day.

i. It is important to understand that the Adam and Eve account is not an optional passage to be accepted or rejected, or allegorized away. According to Paul's theme here in Romans 5, you can't take away the truth of Genesis 3 without taking away principles that lay the foundation for our salvation.

ii. "To Paul, Adam was more than a historical individual, the first man; he was also what his name means in Hebrew - 'humanity.' The whole of humanity is viewed as having existed at first in Adam." (Bruce)

b. **Through one man sin entered the world**: Paul doesn't *prove* this, he simply accepts it true from Genesis 3 - sin **entered the world** through Adam. Significantly, Adam is responsible for the fall of the human race, not Eve. Eve was deceived when she sinned but Adam sinned with full knowledge (1 Timothy 2:14).

c. **And death through sin**: **Death** entered the world and **spread to all men** as a result of Adam's sin. God promised Adam, *in the day that you eat of it you shall surely die* (Genesis 2:17). The principle of death was introduced into the world when Adam sinned and it has reigned on earth ever since. Every grave is mute evidence to the spread and reign of sin since the time of Adam.

d. **Thus death spread to all men, because all sinned**: Since death and sin are connected, we can know that all men are sinners - because all are subject to death. A sinless man is not subject to death, but since every person is subject to death - even the smallest baby - it proves that **all** [mankind] **sinned** in Adam.

i. This sounds odd to our individualistic ears, but Paul clearly teaches that we **all sinned** "in" Adam. Adam is the common father of every person on the earth; every human who has ever lived was "in" Adam's genetic makeup. Therefore, all mankind actually sinned in Adam.

ii. "*All sinned* in this case means 'all sinned in Adam'; Adam's sin is the sin of all." (Morris)

iii. Humans are mortal - subject to death - before they commit any sin themselves. Since mortality is the result of sin, it shows that we are made sinners by Adam's sin, not by our own personal sin.

iv. We may not *like* the fact that we are made sinners by the work of another man. We may protest, and say, "I want to stand on my own two feet, and not be made a sinner because of the work of another man." Nevertheless, it is fair to be made righteous by the work of another man *only* if we are also made sinners by the work of another man. If we aren't made sinners by Adam, then it isn't fair for us to be made righteous by Jesus.

e. **All men**: This truth may make us uncomfortable, but it is still the truth. The smallest baby is a sinner, subject to death. David understood this when he wrote, *Behold, I was brought forth in iniquity, and in sin my mother conceived me* (Psalm 51:5).

i. We can also know that we are *born* sinners for other reasons. First, think of how *selfish* and *angry* the smallest baby can be. Second, think of how we never have to teach our children to be *bad* - they learn that quite on their own, with old Adam teaching the lessons.

ii. If babies are sinners, does that mean that they go to hell? Not necessarily. First, we know that the children of believers are sanctified by the presence of a believing parent (1 Corinthians 7:14). Secondly, David had the assurance that his baby would meet him in heaven (2 Samuel 12:23). Finally, we know that at the end of it all, God, the judge of the entire world, will do right (Genesis 18:25).

iii. If there are the children of unbelieving parents in heaven, it is important to understand that it is not because they are *innocent*. As sons and daughters of guilty Adam, we are each born guilty as well. If such children do go to heaven, it is not because they are innocents who deserve heaven, but because the rich mercy of God has been extended to them as well.

2. (13-14) An objection answered: "I thought we were sinners because we broke the Law."

(For until the law sin was in the world, but sin is not imputed when there is no law. Nevertheless death reigned from Adam to Moses, even over those who had not sinned according to the likeness of the transgression of Adam, who is a type of Him who was to come.

a. **Until the law sin was in the world, but sin is not imputed when there is no law**: We know that at the root of it all we are made sinners because of Adam and not because we break the law ourselves. We know this because sin and death were in the world before the Law was ever given.

i. The law was too late to *prevent* sin and death and it is too weak to *save* from sin and death.

b. **Nevertheless death reigned**: The total, merciless reign of death - even before the law was given at the time of Moses - proves that man was under sin before the law. **Death reigned . . . even over those who had not sinned** in the exact way Adam did, showing that the principle of sin was at work in every human.

c. **Adam, who is a type of Him who was to come**: Paul presents **Adam** as a **type** - a picture, a representation - of Jesus. Both Adam and Jesus were completely sinless men from the beginning, and both of them did things that had consequences for *all* mankind.

3. (15-17) Contrasts between Adam's work and Jesus' work.

But the free gift *is* not like the offense. For if by the one man's offense many died, much more the grace of God and the gift by the grace of the one Man, Jesus Christ, abounded to many. And the gift *is* not like *that which came* through the one who sinned. For the judgment *which came* from one *offense resulted* in condemnation, but the free gift *which came* from many offenses *resulted* in justification. For if by the one man's offense death reigned through the one, much more those who receive abundance of grace and of the gift of righteousness will reign in life through the One, Jesus Christ.)

a. **But the free gift is not like the offense**: Adam gave an **offense** that had consequences for the entire human race - as a result of Adam's **offense, many died**. Jesus gives a **free gift** that has consequences for the entire human race, but in a different way. Through the **free gift** of Jesus, **the grace of God . . . abounded to many**. Adam's work brought death but Jesus' work brings **grace**.

b. **Many died**: This begins to describe the result of Adam's offense. More came: **judgment, resulting in condemnation**, and **death reigned** over men. But there are also the results of Jesus' free gift: grace **abounded to many**, justification (because **many offenses** were laid on Jesus), abundant **grace**, the **gift of righteousness**, and reigning **in life**.

i. "He is not saying that death reigned over us all because we all sinned; he is saying that death reigned over us all because Adam sinned." (Morris)

c. **Death reigned . . . righteousness will reign**: We could say that both Adam and Jesus are kings, each instituting a **reign**. Under Adam, **death reigned**. Under Jesus, we can **reign in life through the One, Jesus Christ**.

i. It is staggering to think how *completely* **death** has **reigned** under Adam. Everyone who is born dies - the mortality rate is 100%. No one survives. When a baby is born, it isn't a question of whether the baby will live or die - it will most certainly die; the only question is *when*. We think of this world as the land of the living, but it is really the land of the dying, and the billions of human bodies cast into the earth over the centuries proves this. But Paul says that the **reign of life** through Jesus is **much more** certain. The believer's **reign in life through** Jesus is *more certain* than death or taxes!

4. (18) Summary: the two men.

Therefore, as through one man's offense *judgment* came to all men, resulting in condemnation, even so through one Man's righteous act *the free gift came* to all men, resulting in justification of life.

a. **One man's offense . . . one Man's righteous act**: From this passage, Adam and Jesus are sometimes known as *the two men*. Between them they represent of all humanity, and everyone is identified in either Adam or Jesus. We are *born* identified with Adam; we may be *born again* into identification with Jesus.

i. The idea of Adam and Jesus as two representatives of the human race is sometimes called *Federal Theology*, or Adam and Jesus are sometimes referred to as *Federal Heads*. This is because under the *federal* system of government, representatives are chosen and the representative speaks for the people who chose him. Adam speaks for those he represents, and Jesus speaks for His people.

ii. Again, someone may object: "But I never *chose* to have Adam represent me." Of course you did! You identified yourself with Adam with the *first sin* you ever committed. It is absolutely true that we were *born* into our identification with Adam, but we *also* choose it with our individual acts of sin.

b. **Resulting in condemnation . . . resulting in justification**: The outcome of this election - choosing Adam or Jesus - means everything. If we choose Adam, we receive **judgment** and **condemnation**. If we choose Jesus, we receive a **free gift** of God's grace and **justification**.

c. **The free gift came to all men**: Does this mean that **all men** are justified by the **free gift**? Without making a personal choice, every person received the curse of Adam's **offense**. Is it therefore true that every person, apart from their personal choice, will receive the benefits of Jesus' obedience? Not at all. First, Paul makes it clear that **the free gift is not like the offense** - they are *not* identical in their result or in their application. Second, over three verses Paul calls the work of Jesus a **free gift**, and he never uses those words to apply to the work of Adam. It is simply the nature of a **gift** that it must be received by faith. Finally, Paul *clearly* teaches throughout the New Testament that all are not saved.

i. In what sense then did **the free gift** come **to all men**? It came in the sense that the **gift** is presented, but not necessarily *received.*

ii. The idea that all men are saved by the work of Jesus whether they know it or not is known as *universalism*. "If the doctrine of universalism is being taught here, Paul would be contradicting himself, for he has already pictured men as perishing because of sin." (Harrison)

5. (19) Summary of the contrasts.

For as by one man's disobedience many were made sinners, so also by one Man's obedience many will be made righteous.

a. **By one man's disobedience**: Adam's **disobedience** makes mankind **sinners**. Jesus' **obedience** makes many **righteous**. Each representative communicates the effect of their work to their "followers."

b. **Many were made sinners**: Paul emphasizes the point again. At the root, we **were made sinners** by the work of Adam. Of course, we chose Adam when we personally sinned. But the principle remains that since another man **made** us **sinners**, we can be **made righteous** by the work of another man.

i. This is the only way for the work of Jesus to benefit us in any way. If every man must stand for himself, without the representation of either Adam or Jesus, then we will all perish. None would be saved, because each of us sins and falls short of the glory of God. Only a sinless person acting on our behalf can save us, and it is fair for Him to act on our behalf because another man put us in this mess by acting on our behalf.

ii. If I robbed a bank and was found guilty of the crime, a friend could not say to the judge, "Your honor, I love my friend and I want to serve his prison time. I will stand in his place and receive the punishment he deserves." The judge would reply, "Nonsense. We will not punish you for his crime. That wouldn't be fair. He did the crime, so he has to pay the penalty." It would only be fair for *another* person to pay the penalty if I were guilty because of *another* person's work.

iii. The person who says, "I don't want to be represented by Adam *or* Jesus; I want to represent myself" doesn't understand two things. First, they don't understand that it really isn't up to us. We didn't make the rules, God did. Secondly, they don't understand that our personal righteousness before God is as *filthy rags* (Isaiah 64:6). To God, our personal righteousness is an offensive counterfeit; so standing for yourself guarantees damnation.

6. (20a) The purpose of the Law.

Moreover the law entered that the offense might abound.

a. **The law entered that the offense might abound**: Paul has shown us that the law does not justify us. Now he shows that in itself, the law doesn't even make us sinners - Adam did that. Then what purpose does the law serve? There is a clear purpose for the law and part of it is so **that the offense might abound**. The law makes man's sin clearer and greater by clearly contrasting it with God's holy standard.

i. The flaws in a precious stone **abound** when contrasted with a perfect stone or when put against a contrasting backdrop. God's perfect law exposes our flaws, and makes our sin **abound**.

b. **Might abound**: There is another way that the **law** makes sin **abound**. Because of the sinfulness of my heart, when I see a line I want to cross it. In this sense, the **law** makes sin **abound** because it draws clear lines between right and wrong that my sinful heart wants to break. Therefore, the law makes me sin more - but not because there is anything wrong in the law, only because something is deeply wrong in the human condition.

7. (20b-21) The reign of grace.

But where sin abounded, grace abounded much more, so that as sin reigned in death, even so grace might reign through righteousness to eternal life through Jesus Christ our Lord.

a. **Where sin abounded, grace abounded much more**: If **sin abounded** under the law, then **grace abounded much more** under Jesus. Literally, the phrase **abounded much more** means "super-abounded." God makes His grace *super-abound* over abounding sin!

i. We might have expected that **where sin abounded**, God's *anger* or *judgment* would have **abounded much more**. But God's love is so amazing that **grace abounded much more** where we might have expected wrath.

ii. If grace *super-abounds* over sin, then we know that it is impossible to *out-sin* the grace of God. We can't sin more than God can forgive, but we can reject His grace and forgiveness.

b. **Even so grace might reign**: As Paul stated before, **sin reigned in death**. But **grace** reigns also. The reign of grace is marked by **righteousness** and **eternal life** and is **through Jesus**.

i. **Grace** reigns **through righteousness**. Many people have the idea that where grace reigns, there will be a disregard for **righteousness** and a casual attitude towards sin. But that isn't the reign of grace at all. Paul wrote in another letter what grace teaches us: *For the grace of God that brings salvation has appeared to all men, teaching us that, denying ungodliness and worldly lusts, we should live soberly, righteously, and godly in the present age* (Titus 2:11-12). **Grace** reigns **through righteousness**, and **grace** teaches righteousness.

ii. **Grace** reigns **to eternal life**. God's grace gives us something and takes us somewhere. It gives more than never-ending life. **Eternal life** has the idea of a *present quality of life*, God's quality of life, given to us right now - not simply when we die.

iii. **Grace** reigns **through Jesus**. There is a King in the kingdom where grace reigns, and the King is Jesus. A life of grace is all about Jesus and others, and not about me. A life of grace doesn't look to self because it understands that this undeserved favor of God is given apart from any reason in self. All the reasons are in Jesus; none of the reasons are in myself. Grace doesn't reign through self, but **through Jesus**.

c. **Even so grace might reign through righteousness**: Wherever grace rules, God's righteous standard will be respected. The legalist's fear is that the reign of grace will provide wicked hearts with a license to sin, but Scripture doesn't share that fear. Grace does not accommodate sin, it faces it squarely and goes above sin in order to conquer it. Grace does not wink at unrighteousness, it confronts sin with the atonement at the cross and the victory won at the open tomb.

i. Grace is no friend to sin; it is its sworn enemy. "As heat is opposed to cold, and light to darkness, so grace is opposed to sin. Fire and water may as well agree in the same vessel as grace and sin in the same heart." (Thomas Benton Brooks)

ii. In John Bunyan's classic *Pilgrim's Progress*, a wonderful character is named "Mr. Honest." He traveled the pilgrim's way and saw many a fellow pilgrim - some who set out boldly and strongly but who turned back. He saw others who stumbled at the start but finished in fine fashion. Some began full of faith but ended in doubt, and others came to greater assurance along the pilgrim's road. Mr. Honest obviously knew a lot about the journey of the Christian life and he summed up all his knowledge in his last words:

"Mr. Honest called for his friends, and said unto them 'I die, but shall make no will. As for my honesty, it shall go with me' . . . When the day that he was to be gone was come, he addressed himself to go over the river. Now the river at that time overflowed the banks in some places, but Mr. Honest in his lifetime had spoken to one [named] Good-conscience to meet him there, that which he also did, and lent him his hand, and so helped him over. The last words of Mr. Honest were, *'Grace reigns!'* So he left the world."

Romans 6 - Made Safe for Grace

A. The believer under grace and the problem of habitual sin.

1. (1) Should we live a life of sin so we can receive more grace?

What shall we say then? Shall we continue in sin that grace may abound?

a. **Shall we continue in sin that grace may abound?** Paul introduced the idea that *where sin abounded, grace abounded much more* (Romans 5:20). He now wonders if someone might take this truth to imply that it doesn't matter if a Christian lives a life of sin, because God will always overcome greater sin with greater grace.

i. After all, if God loves sinners, then why worry about sin? If God gives grace to sinners, then why not sin more and receive more grace? Some people think that their job is to sin and God's job is to forgive, so they will do their job and God will do His job!

ii. In the early part of the 20th century the Russian monk Gregory Rasputin taught and lived the idea of salvation through repeated experiences of sin and repentance. He believed that because those who sin the most require the most forgiveness, therefore a sinner who continues to sin without restraint enjoys more of God's grace (when he repents for the moment) than the ordinary sinner. Therefore, Rasputin lived in notorious sin and taught that this was the way to salvation. This is an extreme example of the idea behind Paul's question "**Shall we continue in sin that grace may abound?**"

iii. But in a less extreme way, the question still confronts us. Is the plan of grace "safe"? Won't people abuse grace? If God's salvation and approval are given on the basis of faith instead of works, won't we just *say* "I believe" and then live any way we please?

iv. From a purely natural or secular viewpoint, *grace is dangerous*. This is why many people don't really teach or believe in grace and instead emphasize living by law. They believe that if you tell people that God saves and accepts them apart from what they deserve, then they will have no motive to be obedient. In their opinion, you simply can't keep people on the straight and narrow without a threat from God hanging over their head. If they believe their position in Jesus is settled because of what Jesus did, then the motivation of holy living is gone.

b. **Shall we continue in sin**: The verb tense of the phrase **continue in sin** (the *present active* tense) makes it clear that Paul describes the *practice of habitual sin*. In this first part of Romans 6, Paul writes about someone who remains in a lifestyle of sin, thinking that it is acceptable so **that grace may abound**.

2. (2) A life of sin is unacceptable because our death to sin changes our relationship to sin.

Certainly not! How shall we who died to sin live any longer in it?

a. **Certainly not!** For Paul, the idea that anyone might *continue in sin that grace may abound* is unthinkable. **Certainly not** is a strong phrase. It might also be translated, "Perish the thought!" Or, "Away with the notion!"

b. **How shall we who died to sin live any longer in it?** Paul establishes an important principle. When we are born again, when we have believed on Jesus for our salvation, our relationship with sin is permanently changed. We have **died to sin**. Therefore, if we have **died to sin**, then we should not **live any longer in it**. It simply isn't fitting to **live any longer in** something you have **died to**.

c. **We who died to sin**: At this point, Paul has much to explain about what exactly he means by **died to sin**, but the general point is clear - Christians have died to sin, and they should no longer live in it. Before, we were dead *in* sin (Ephesians 2:1); now we are dead **to sin**.

3. (3-4) The illustration of the believer's death to sin: baptism.

Or do you not know that as many of us as were baptized into Christ Jesus were baptized into His death? Therefore we were buried with Him through baptism into death, that just as Christ was raised from the dead by the glory of the Father, even so we also should walk in newness of life.

a. **Or do you not know**: The implication is that Paul is dealing with fundamental concepts that every Christians should know.

b. **As many of us as were baptized into Christ Jesus**: The idea behind the ancient Greek word for **baptized** is "to immerse or overwhelm something." The Bible uses this idea of being **baptized** into something in several different ways. When a person is **baptized** in water, they are immersed or covered over with water. When they are **baptized** *with the Holy Spirit*

(Matthew 3:11, Acts 1:5), they are "immersed" or "covered over" with the Holy Spirit. When they are **baptized** with suffering (Mark 10:39), they are "immersed" or "covered over" with suffering. Here, Paul refers to being **baptized** - "immersed" or "covered over" - in **Christ Jesus**.

c. **Therefore we were buried with Him through baptism into death, that just as Christ was raised from the dead**: Water baptism (being **baptized into Christ**) is a dramatization or "acting out" of the believer's "immersion" or identification with Jesus in His death and resurrection.

> i. "From this and other references to baptism in Paul's writings, it is plain that he did not regard baptism as an 'optional extra' in the Christian life." (Bruce)

d. **We were buried with Him . . . as Christ was raised from the dead by the glory of the Father, even so we also should walk in newness of life**: Paul also builds on the idea of going under the water as a picture of being **buried** and coming up from the water as a picture of rising from the dead.

> i. Of course, baptism also has the association of *cleansing*, but that isn't particularly relevant to Paul's point here.

> ii. In this regard, baptism is important as an illustration of spiritual reality, but it does not make that reality come to pass. If someone has not spiritually died and risen with Jesus, all the baptisms in the world will not accomplish it for them.

> iii. But Paul's point is clear: something dramatic and life changing happened in the life of the believer. You can't die and rise again without it changing your life. The believer has a real (although spiritual) death and resurrection with Jesus Christ.

4. (5-10) Considering the implications of our death and resurrection with Jesus.

For if we have been united together in the likeness of His death, certainly we also shall be *in the likeness* of *His* resurrection, knowing this, that our old man was crucified with *Him,* that the body of sin might be done away with, that we should no longer be slaves of sin. For he who has died has been freed from sin. Now if we died with Christ, we believe that we shall also live with Him, knowing that Christ, having been raised from the dead, dies no more. Death no longer has dominion over Him. For *the death* that He died, He died to sin once for all; but *the life* that He lives, He lives to God.

a. **United together**: This expresses a close union. The phrase "exactly expresses the process by which a graft becomes united with the life of a tree . . . The union is of the closest sort, and life from Christ flows through to him" (Morris). This fits in with Jesus' picture of abiding from John 15.

i. This close union is *both* in **His death** and in **His resurrection**. God has both experiences for us. Paul expressed a similar idea for his own life in Philippians 3:10-11: *that I may know Him and the power of His resurrection, and the fellowship of His sufferings, being conformed to His death, if, by any means, I may attain to the resurrection from the dead.* Some are all too ready to be **united together** in the glory of resurrection, but are unwilling to be **united together** in **His death**.

b. **Certainly we also shall be in the likeness of His resurrection**: Our participation in the death of Jesus makes our participation in His resurrection certain.

i. It is too easy for some Christians to focus solely on the "crucified life," failing to see that it is a part (and an essential part) of a bigger picture: preparation for *resurrection* life.

c. **Knowing this, that our old man was crucified with Him**: The death of the **old man** is an established fact. It happened spiritually when we were identified with Jesus' death at our salvation.

i. The **old man** is the self that is patterned after Adam, the part of us deeply ingrained in rebellion against God and His commands. The system of law is unable to deal with the **old man**, because it can only tell the **old man** what the righteous standard of God is. The law tries to reform the **old man**, to get him to "turn over a new leaf." But the system of grace understands that the **old man** can never be reformed. He must be put to death, and for the believer the **old man** dies with Jesus on the cross.

ii. The crucifixion of the **old man** is something that God did in us. None of us nailed the **old man** to the cross. Jesus did it, and we are told to account it as being done. "In us there was nothing even to sicken and to weaken our old man, much less to murder him by crucifixion; God had to do this." (Lenski)

iii. In place of the **old man**, God gives the believer a *new man* - a self that is instinctively obedient and pleasing to God; this aspect of our person is that which was raised with Christ in His resurrection. The New Testament describes the *new man* for us.

The new man, which was created according to God, in righteousness and true holiness (Ephesians 4:24).

The new man who is renewed in knowledge according to the image of Him who created him (Colossians 3:10).

d. **That the body of sin might be done away with**: God uses our death to the **old man**, the sin nature, to liberate us from sin. A dead man can no longer have authority over us, so we are to remember and account the **old man** as **crucified with Him**.

i. The two other places in the New Testament which mention the **old man** remind us to consider him done away with, telling us to *put off* the old man as something dead and gone (Ephesians 4:22 and Colossians 3:9). Strictly speaking, we don't *battle* the **old man**. We simply reckon him as dead.

ii. "Evil enters us now as an interloper and a stranger, and works sad havoc, but it does not abide in us upon the throne; it is an alien, and despised, and no more honored and delighted in. We are dead to the reigning power of sin." (Spurgeon)

e. **Done away with**: If the **old man** is dead, why do I feel a pull to sin inside? It comes from the *flesh*, which is distinct from the **old man**. It's hard to precisely describe the flesh; some have called it "the screen on which the inner man is displayed." Our inner being has desires and impulses and passions; these are played out in our *mind*, in our *will*, and in our *emotions*. The *flesh* is what acts out the inner man.

i. The flesh is a problem in the battle against sin because it has been expertly trained in sinful habits by three sources. First, the **old man**, before he was crucified with Christ, trained and "imprinted" himself on the flesh. Second, the *world system*, in its spirit of rebellion against God, can have a continuing influence on the flesh. Finally, the *devil* seeks to tempt and influence the flesh towards sin.

ii. With the **old man** dead, what do we do with the flesh? God calls us, in participation with Him, to actively do day by day with the flesh just what He has already done with the old man - to crucify it, make it dead to sin (Galatians 5:24). But when we allow the flesh to be continually influenced by the old man's habits of the past, the world, and the devil, the flesh will exert a powerful pull towards sin. If we let the *new man* within us influence the mind, the will, and the emotions, then we will find the battle less intense.

f. **That we should no longer be slaves of sin. For he who has died has been freed from sin**: Our slavery to sin can only be broken by death. In the 1960 film *Spartacus*, Kirk Douglas played the escaped slave Spartacus, who led a brief but widespread slave rebellion in ancient Rome. At one point in the movie Spartacus says: "Death is the only freedom a slave knows. That's why he is not afraid of it." We are set free from sin because the old man has died with Jesus on the cross. Now a new man, a free man, lives.

g. **Having been raised from the dead, dies no more. Death no longer has dominion over Him**: Since we have already died to sin with Jesus,

death no longer has dominion over us. The new man not only has life; he has *eternal* life.

h. **The life that he lives, he lives to God**: The new life we are granted isn't given so we can live unto ourselves. With the new life, **he lives to God**. We aren't dead to sin, free from sin, and given eternal life to live as we please, but to live to please God.

> i. "If God has given to you and to me an entirely new life in Christ, how can that new life spend itself after the fashion of the old life? Shall the spiritual live as the carnal? How can you that were the servants of sin, but have been made free by precious blood, go back to your old slavery?" (Spurgeon)

> ii. This change in the life of the one who is born again was understood and predicted as a feature of God's New Covenant, where because of new hearts our innermost being *wants* to do God's will and be slaves to righteousness (Ezekiel 36:26-27).

> iii. The eleventh of the original 42 articles of Church of England states this truth with a beauty that Sixteenth Century English expresses well: "The grace of Christ, or the holie Ghost by him geven, dothe take awaie the stonie harte, and geveth an harte of flesh." God takes away our rock-like heart and gives us a soft heart of flesh.

5. (11-12) Practical application of the principle of our death and resurrection with Jesus.

Likewise you also, reckon yourselves to be dead indeed to sin, but alive to God in Christ Jesus our Lord. Therefore do not let sin reign in your mortal body, that you should obey it in its lusts.

a. **Reckon yourselves to be dead indeed to sin: Reckon** is an accounting word. Paul tells us to *account* or to **reckon** the old man as forever dead. God never calls us to "crucify" the old man, but instead to account him as already dead because of our identification with Jesus' death on the cross.

b. **Reckon yourselves to be . . . alive to God in Christ Jesus our Lord**: The death to sin is only one side of the equation. The old man is gone, but the new man lives on (as described in Romans 6:4-5).

c. **Therefore do not let sin reign in your mortal body**: This is something that can only be said to the Christian, to the one who has had the old man crucified with Christ and has been given a new man in Jesus. Only the person set free from sin can be told, **"do not let sin reign."**

> i. The Christian is the one truly set free. The man or woman who isn't converted yet is free to sin, but they are not free to stop sinning and live righteously, because of the tyranny of the old man.

ii. In Jesus, we are truly set free and are offered the opportunity to obey the natural inclination of the new man - which wants to please God and honor Him.

d. **Therefore do not let sin reign**: The old man is dead, and there is new life - *free from sin* - in Jesus. Yet, many Christians never *experience* this freedom. Because of unbelief, self-reliance, or ignorance, many Christians never live in the freedom Jesus paid for on the cross.

i. D. L. Moody used to speak of an old black woman in the South following the Civil War. Being a former slave, she was confused about her status and asked: "Now is I free, or been I not? When I go to my old master he says I ain't free, and when I go to my own people they say I is, and I don't know whether I'm free or not. Some people told me that Abraham Lincoln signed a proclamation, but master says he didn't; he didn't have any right to."

ii. This is exactly the place many Christians are. They are, and have been, legally set free from their slavery to sin, yet they are unsure of that truth. The following verses give practical help in living out the freedom Jesus has granted us.

6. (13-14) How to walk in the freedom Jesus has given us.

And do not present your members *as* instruments of unrighteousness to sin, but present yourselves to God as being alive from the dead, and your members *as* instruments of righteousness to God. For sin shall not have dominion over you, for you are not under law but under grace.

a. **Do not present your members as instruments of unrighteousness to sin, but present yourselves to God**: A person can be "officially" set free, yet still imprisoned. If a person lives in prison for years, and then is set free, they often still think and act like a prisoner. The habits of freedom aren't ingrained in their life yet. Here, Paul shows how to build the habits of freedom in the Christian life.

i. In the fourteenth century two brothers fought for the right to rule over a dukedom in what is now Belgium. The elder brother's name was Raynald, but he was commonly called "Crassus," a Latin nickname meaning "fat," for he was horribly obese. After a heated battle, Raynald's younger brother Edward led a successful revolt against him and assumed the title of Duke over his lands. But instead of killing Raynald, Edward devised a curious imprisonment. He had a room in the castle built around "Crassus," a room with only one door. The door was not locked, the windows were not barred, and Edward promised Raynald that he could regain his land and his title any time that he wanted to. All he would have to do is leave the room. The obstacle to freedom was not in the doors or the windows, but with Raynald himself. Being grossly overweight, he could not fit through the door, even though it was of near-normal size. All Raynald needed to do was diet down to a smaller size, then walk out a free man, with all he had before his fall. However, his younger brother kept sending him an assortment of tasty foods, and Raynald's desire to be free never won out over his desire to eat. Some would accuse Duke Edward of being cruel to his older brother, but he would simply reply, "My brother is not a prisoner. He may leave when he so wills." But Raynald stayed in that room for ten years, until Edward himself was killed in battle.

ii. This accurately illustrates the experience of many Christians. Jesus set them forever free legally, and they may walk in that freedom from sin whenever they choose. But since they keep yielding their bodily appetites to the service of sin, they live a life of defeat, discouragement, and imprisonment.

b. **Do not present your members as instruments of unrighteousness to sin**: This is the first key to walking in the freedom Jesus won for us. We must *not* present the parts of our body to the service of sin. The New Living Translation communicates the idea well: *Do not let any part of your body become a tool of wickedness, to be used for sinning.*

i. Your **members** are the parts of your body - your ears, lips, eyes, hands, mind, and so forth. The idea is very practical: "You have eyes. Do not put them in the service of sin. You have ears. Do not put them in the service of sin."

ii. **Instruments** could be better-translated *weapons*. The parts of our body are weapons in the battle for right living. When the parts of our body are given over to righteousness, they are *weapons* for good. When they are given over to sin, they are *weapons* for evil.

iii. An example of this is how God used David's hands to slay Goliath in the cause of righteousness. Later, sin used David's eyes for unrighteousness when he looked upon Bathsheba.

c. **But present yourselves to God**: This is the second key to walking in the freedom Jesus won for us. It isn't enough to take the weapons away from the service of sin. They must then be enlisted in the service of righteousness - and, as in any warfare, the side with superior weapons usually wins.

i. The idea is similar to the manner in which the priests in the Old Testament consecrated their bodies to God. Sacrificial blood was applied to the ear, to the thumb, and on the big toe, showing that those parts of their body (and all other parts) belonged to God and were to be used for His glory (Exodus 29:20).

ii. We present ourselves to God **as being alive from the dead**. This first has the idea that all connection with the previous life - the old man - must be done away with. That life is dead and gone. Secondly, it has the idea of obligation, because we owe everything to the One who has given us new life!

d. **For sin shall not have dominion over you**: Spurgeon said that these words give us a *test*, a *promise*, and an *encouragement*.

i. It is a *test* of our claim to be Christians. Does anger have dominion over you? Does murmuring and complaining? Does covetousness have dominion over you? Does pride? Does laziness have dominion over you? If sin has dominion over us, we should seriously ask if we are really converted.

ii. It is a *promise* of victory. It doesn't say that "sin will not be present in us," because that will only be fulfilled when we are resurrected in glory. But it does promise that sin will not have *dominion* over us because of the great work Jesus did in us when we were born again.

iii. It is an *encouragement* for hope and strength in the battle against sin. God hasn't condemned you under the dominion of sin - He has set you free in Jesus. This is encouragement for the Christian struggling against sin, for the new Christian, and for the backslider.

e. **For you are not under law but under grace**: This is the path, the means, by which we can live in this freedom. It will never happen in a legalistic, performance oriented Christian life. It will happen as we live **not under law but under grace**.

i. **Law** clearly defined God's standard, and shows us where we fall short of it. But it cannot give the freedom from sin that **grace** provides. Remember that *grace reigns through righteousness* (Romans 5:21). Grace, not law provides the freedom and the power to live over sin.

ii. This shows again that a life lived truly under grace will be a righteous life. Grace is never a license to sin. "To treat being *under grace* as an excuse for sinning is a sign that one is not really *under grace* at all." (Bruce)

f. **Not under law but under grace**: This is another way to describe the radical change in the life of someone who is born again. For the Jewish person of Paul's day, living life **under law** was everything. The **law** was the way to God's approval and eternal life. Now, Paul shows that in light of the New Covenant, we are **not under law but under grace**. His work in our life has changed everything.

i. Paul has answered his question from Romans 6:1. Why don't we just continue in habitual sin so grace may abound? Because when we are saved, when our sins are forgiven, and God's grace is extended to us, we are radically changed. The old man is dead, and the new man lives.

ii. In light of these remarkable changes, it is utterly incompatible for a new creation in Jesus to be comfortable in habitual sin. A state of sin can only be temporary for the Christian. As Spurgeon is credited with saying: "The grace that does not change my life will not save my soul."

iii. John states the same idea in another way: *Whoever abides in Him does not* [habitually] *sin. Whoever* [habitually] *sins has neither seen Him nor known Him . . . Whoever has been born of God does not* [habitually] *sin, for his seed remains in him; and he cannot* [habitually] *sin, because he has been born of God* (1 John 3:6 and 3:9).

iv. The changes may not come all at one time, and they may not come to each area of one's life at the same time, but they will be there and they will be real and they will be increasing as time goes on.

g. **Under grace**: God makes us "safe" for grace by *changing* us as we receive His grace; He sets us free and equips us to live righteously before Him. Once dead to sin, it is unthinkable to continue our former practice of sin. Once the caterpillar has been made a butterfly, the butterfly has no business crawling around on trees and leaves like a caterpillar again.

i. "God has so changed your nature by his grace that when you sin you shall be like a fish on dry land, you shall be out of your element, and long to get into a right state again. You cannot sin, for you love God. The sinner may drink sin down as the ox drinketh down water, but to you it shall be as the brine of the sea. You may become so foolish as to try the pleasures of the world, but they shall be no pleasures to you." (Spurgeon)

B. The believer under grace and the problem of occasional sin.

1. (15) A new question is asked: shall we sin (occasionally) because we are not under law but under grace?

What then? Shall we sin because we are not under law but under grace? Certainly not!

a. **Shall we sin because we are not under law but under grace?** Paul has convinced us that a lifestyle of habitual sin is not compatible with one whose life is changed by grace. But what about an occasional sin here and there? If we are under grace and not law, must we be so concerned about a little sin here and there?

b. **Shall we sin**: Again, the verb tense of the ancient Greek word **sin** is important (the *aorist active* tense). It indicates dabbling in sin, not the continual habitual sin described in the question of Romans 6:1.

i. "The verb in verse one is in the present subjunctive, speaking of habitual, continuous action. The verb in verse fifteen is in the aorist subjunctive, referring to a single act." (Wuest)

2. (16-17) Spiritual principles we need to understand in order to answer the question.

Do you not know that to whom you present yourselves slaves to obey, you are that one's slaves whom you obey, whether of sin *leading* to death, or of obedience *leading* to righteousness? But God be thanked that *though* you were slaves of sin, yet you obeyed from the heart that form of doctrine to which you were delivered.

a. **To whom you present yourselves slaves to obey, you are that one's slaves**: Whatever you present yourself to obey, you become its slave. For example, if I obey my appetite constantly, I am a slave to it. So we have a choice in our slavery: **sin leading to death** or **obedience leading to righteousness**.

i. One way or another, we will serve somebody. The option to live our life without serving either **sin** or **obedience** isn't open to us.

b. **Though you were slaves of sin**: Paul puts it in the past tense because we *have been* freed from our slavery to sin. He also says that we have been set free by *faith*, which he describes as **obedience from the heart**. The faith is put in *God's Word*, which he describes as **that form of doctrine**. All in all, the point is clear: "You put your faith in God and His Word, and now you are set free. Now live every day consistent with that freedom."

i. As was seen earlier in Romans 6, we can be *legally* free and still *choose* to live like a prisoner. Paul has a simple command and encouragement for the Christian: *be* what you *are*.

ii. **Obeyed from the heart** is a wonderful description of faith. It shows that faith comes from the **heart**, not only the mind. It shows that faith results in **obedience** because if we really believe something, we will act according to that belief.

c. **That form of doctrine**: This phrase is part of a beautiful picture. The word **form** describes a mold used to shape molten metal. The idea is that God wants to *shape* us - first He *melts* us by the work of the Holy Spirit and the Word of God. Then He *pours us* into His mold of truth - **that form of doctrine** and shapes us into His image.

i. Adam Clarke on **that form of doctrine**: "Here Christianity is represented under the notion of a *mould*, or *die*, into which they were *cast*, and from which they took the *impression* of its excellence. The *figure* upon this *die* is the image of God, *righteousness and true holiness*, which was *stamped* on their souls in believing the Gospel and receiving the

Holy Ghost. The words . . . refer to the *melting of metal*, which, when it is liquefied, is cast into the mould, that it may receive the impression that is *sunk* or *cut* in the mould; and therefore the words may be literally translated, *into which mould of doctrine ye have been cast.* They were *melted* down under the preaching of the word, and then were capable of receiving the stamp of its purity."

3. (18) Why not then, occasionally sin? Because sin is not our master, and we no longer serve it.

And having been set free from sin, you became slaves of righteousness.

a. **Having been set free from sin**: What does it mean to be **free from sin** and to become a slave **of righteousness**? It means that sin is no longer your boss or your master. Now **righteousness** is your boss, so serve **righteousness** instead of sin. It isn't right to think about pleasing your old boss when you change jobs.

b. **Slaves of righteousness**: What does it mean to be a slave? A slave was more than an employee. The noted Greek scholar Kenneth Wuest defined the ancient Greek word for a **slave** here by these terms:

- One born into a condition of slavery

- One whose will is swallowed up in the will of another

- One who is bound to the master with bonds only death can break

- One who serves his master to the disregard of his own interests

i. The following *was once* true in regard to our slavery to sin:

- We were born as slaves to sin

- Our will was swallowed up and captive to sin within us

- Our bondage to sin was so strong that only death - spiritually dying with Jesus on the cross - could break the bondage

- We were so enslaved to sin that we served it to the disregard of our own interest, even when sin destroyed us

ii. Now the following *is true* in regard to our slavery to righteousness:

- We are born again, now as **slaves to righteousness**

- Our will is now swallowed up in the will of God. It is His will that matters to us, not our own

- We are bound to Jesus with bonds that only death can break; but since He has triumphed over death and given us eternal life, those bonds will *never* be broken!

- We now willingly chose serve Jesus to the disregard of our own (selfish) interests

c. **Set free from sin**: This means that we never *have* to sin again. Though sin is inevitable until our flesh is resurrected in glory, it isn't because God has designed a system by which we *must* sin.

> i. Sinless perfection in this body is an illusion. 1 John 1:8 makes this clear: *If we say we have no sin, we deceive ourselves, and the truth is not in us.* Yet we know that in the power of Jesus we each can resist the *next* temptation - and that is what Jesus wants us to be concerned with.

> ii. "Because of the frailty of man, the Christian at infrequent intervals does yield to the evil nature and sin. *But the point is, God has so constituted him, that he need not do so.*" (Wuest)

> iii. It is mockery to tell a slave, "Don't behave as a slave" - but you can say that to someone who is set free. Jesus Christ tells us to no longer behave as if we were slaves to sin. We have been set free; now we are to *think* and *live* as free people.

4. (19-23) How to keep from enslaving ourselves.

I speak in human *terms* because of the weakness of your flesh. For just as you presented your members *as* slaves of uncleanness, and of lawlessness *leading* to *more* lawlessness, so now present your members *as* slaves *of* righteousness for holiness. For when you were slaves of sin, you were free in regard to righteousness. What fruit did you have then in the things of which you are now ashamed? For the end of those things *is* death. But now having been set free from sin, and having become slaves of God, you have your fruit to holiness, and the end, everlasting life. For the wages of sin *is* death, but the gift of God *is* eternal life in Christ Jesus our Lord.

a. **I speak in human terms because of the weakness of your flesh**: The Apostle Paul apologized for using slavery as an illustration, because it was so degrading and pervasive, and especially because many of his Roman readers were slaves. Yet he knew this was an accurate and meaningful illustration.

b. **You presented your members . . . so now present**: Paul repeats a point made earlier. First, **present your members as slaves of righteousness**. This means that we don't show up for work to our old boss.

> i. Can you imagine? A new job, and the first day on the new job you leave work at lunch time and go to your old job and ask your old boss what he wants you to do. It just isn't right!

c. **Lawlessness leading to more lawlessness**: Paul describes a principle ingrained in human nature. **Lawlessness** leads **to more lawlessness. Righteousness** leads to **holiness** - which is more righteousness. This describes the dynamic power of our habits and how we move along in the direction we are pointed.

i. Think of four trees in a row: the first at one year of growth, the second at five years, the third at ten years, and the last at 15 years. Which tree will be the most difficult to pull up out of the ground? Obviously, the longer we are *rooted* in a behavior the harder it is to uproot it - a principle that works both for good and evil.

d. **For when you were slaves of sin, you were free in regard to righteousness**: Paul's point is almost humorous. When we were **slaves of sin**, we were free all right - **free in regard to righteousness**. Some freedom!

e. **What fruit did you have then**: To walk in victory over sin we must think rightly about the **fruit** of sin. To say, "**The end of those things is death**" means that the end product of sin is death - not fun. But the end product of righteousness is **everlasting life**.

i. In a time of temptation, these truths can seem unreal - so we must rely on God's Word. When we are tempted, faith reminds us of the bitter fruit of sin when our feelings may forget that bitter fruit.

f. **For the wages of sin is death, but the gift of God is eternal life in Christ Jesus our Lord**: When you work for sin, your wages are **death**. When we serve God we get no pay - but He freely gives us the best benefit package imaginable.

i. **Wages of sin**: "Every sinner *earns* this by long, sore, and painful service. O! What pains do men take to get to hell! Early and late they toil at sin; and would not Divine justice be in their *debt*, if it did not pay them their due wages?" (Clarke)

i. Answering his question from Romans 6:15, Paul has made it clear: As believers, we have a change of ownership. The Christian must fight against even occasional sin because we need to work for and work under our new Master. It isn't appropriate for us to work for our old master.

Romans 7 - Exposing the Weakness of the Law

A. Dead to the Law.

1. (1-3) The law has authority only over the living.

Or do you not know, brethren (for I speak to those who know the law), that the law has dominion over a man as long as he lives? For the woman who has a husband is bound by the law to *her* husband as long as he lives. But if the husband dies, she is released from the law of *her* husband. So then if, while *her* husband lives, she marries another man, she will be called an adulteress; but if her husband dies, she is free from that law, so that she is no adulteress, though she has married another man.

a. **The law has dominion**: In Romans 6:14, Paul told us that *you are not under law but under grace.* After the discussion in Romans 6:15-23 regarding practical implications of this, he now explains more completely how it is that we are no longer under the dominion of the law.

b. **That the law has dominion over a man**: The ancient Greek wording here has no word "**the**" before **law**. This means Paul speaks of a principle broader than the Mosaic Law. The **law** that has **dominion** over man includes the Law of Moses, but there is a broader principle of law communicated by creation and by conscience, and these also have **dominion over a man**.

c. **The law has dominion over a man as long as he lives**: Paul makes the point that death ends all obligations and contracts. A wife is no longer bound to her husband if he dies because death ends that contract. **If her husband dies, she is free from that law.**

2. (4) Our death with Jesus sets us free from the law.

Therefore, my brethren, you also have become dead to the law through the body of Christ, that you may be married to another; to Him who was raised from the dead, that we should bear fruit to God.

a. **You also have become dead to the law through the body of Christ**: In Romans 6:3-8, Paul carefully explained that we died with Jesus and we also rose with Him, although Paul there only spoke of our death to *sin*. Now he explains that we also died to the **law**.

i. Some might think, "Yes, we were saved by grace, but we must *live by law* to please God." Here Paul makes it plain that believers are **dead to the law** as far as it represents a *principle of living* or a *place of right standing* before God.

ii. "Believers are through with the law. It is not for them an option as a way of salvation. They do not seek to be right with God by obeying some form of law, as the adherents of almost all religions have done." (Morris)

b. **That you may be married to another**: However, we are not free from the law so we can live unto ourselves. We are free so we can be "**married**" to Jesus and so that we can **bear fruit to God**.

3. (5) The problem with the law.

For when we were in the flesh, the sinful passions which were aroused by the law were at work in our members to bear fruit to death.

a. **When we were in the flesh**: Under the law, we did not *bear fruit to God*. Instead we bore **fruit to death**, because the law **aroused** the **passions** of sins within us.

b. **To bear fruit to death**: Paul will explain this problem of the law more fully in Romans 7:7-14. But now we see his point - that we only come fully to the place of *bearing fruit for God* when we are free from the law.

4. (6) Delivered from the law.

But now we have been delivered from the law, having died to what we were held by, so that we should serve in the newness of the Spirit and not *in* the oldness of the letter.

a. **But now we have been delivered from the law**: Here Paul summarizes the theme of Romans 7:1-5. Because we died with Jesus at Calvary, we are dead to the law and **delivered** from its dominion over us as a principle of *justification* or of *sanctification*.

i. The law does not *justify* us; it does not make us right with God. The law does not *sanctify* us; it does not take us deeper with God and make us more holy before Him.

b. **So that we should serve in the newness of the Spirit**: Our freedom is not given so we can stop serving God but so that we can serve Him better, under the **newness of the Spirit and not in the oldness of the letter**.

i. How well do you **serve in the newness of the Spirit**? It is a shame that many serve sin or legalism with more devotion than those who should serve God out of the **newness of the Spirit**. It is unfortunate when fear motivates us more than love.

B. Our problem with God's perfect law.

1. (7a) Paul asks: **Is the law** (equal to) **sin**?

What shall we say then? *Is* **the law sin?**

a. **Is the law sin?** If we follow the train of thought we can understand how someone might infer this. Paul insisted that we must die to the law if we will bear fruit to God. Someone must think, "Surely there is something wrong with the law!"

2. (7b) No, the law is *good* because it reveals sin to us.

Certainly not! On the contrary, I would not have known sin except through the law. For I would not have known covetousness unless the law had said, "You shall not covet."

a. **I would not have known sin except through the law**: The law is like an x-ray machine; it reveals what is there but hidden. You can't blame an x-ray for what it exposes.

b. **For I would not have known covetousness unless the law had said, "You shall not covet."** The law sets the "speed limit" so we know exactly if we are going too fast. We might never know that we are sinning in many areas (such as **covetousness**) if the law didn't show us specifically.

3. (8) Sin corrupts the commandment (law).

But sin, taking opportunity by the commandment, produced in me all *manner of evil* **desire. For apart from the law sin** *was* **dead.**

a. **But sin, taking opportunity by the commandments**: Paul describes the dynamic where the warning "Don't do that!" may become a call to action because of our sinful, rebellious hearts. It isn't the fault of the **commandment**, but it is our fault.

i. In his book *Confessions*, the great theologian of the ancient church Augustine described how this dynamic worked in his life as a young man: "There was a pear tree near our vineyard, laden with fruit. One stormy night we rascally youths set out to rob it and carry our spoils away. We took off a huge load of pears - not to feast upon ourselves, but to throw them to the pigs, though we ate just enough to have the pleasure of forbidden fruit. They were nice pears, but it was not the pears that my wretched soul coveted, for I had plenty better at home. I picked them simply in order to become a thief. The only feast I got was a feast of iniquity, and that I enjoyed to the full. What was it that I loved in the theft? Was it the pleasure of acting against the law? The desire to steal was awakened simply by the prohibition of stealing."

ii. In American history, we know that the Prohibition Act didn't stop drinking. In many ways it made drinking more attractive to people because of our desire to break boundaries set by the commandment.

iii. Once God draws a boundary for us, we are immediately enticed to cross that boundary - which is no fault of God or His boundary, but the fault of our sinful hearts.

b. **Sin, taking opportunity by the commandment**: The weakness of the law isn't in the law - it is in us. Our hearts are so wicked that they can find **opportunity** for **all manner of evil desire** from something good like the law of God.

i. "The word *opportunity* in the original is a military term meaning a base of operations. Prohibition furnishes a springboard from which sin is all too ready to take off." (Harrison)

ii. A waterfront hotel in Florida was concerned that people might try to fish from the balconies so they put up signs saying, "NO FISH-ING FROM THE BALCONY." They had constant problems with people fishing from the balconies, with lines and sinker weights break-ing windows and bothering people in rooms below. They finally solved the problem by simply taking down the signs - and no one thought to fish from the balconies. Because of our fallen nature, the law can actually work like an invitation to sin.

c. **Apart from the law, sin was dead**: This shows how great the evil of sin is - it can take something good and holy like the law and twist it to promote evil. Sin warps love into lust, an honest desire to provide for one's family into greed, and the law into a promoter of sin.

4. (9) Paul's state of innocence before he knew the law.

I was alive once without the law, but when the commandment came, sin revived and I died.

a. **I was alive once without the law**: Children can be innocent before they know or understand what law requires. This is what Paul refers to when he says **I was alive once without the law**.

i. "He is not alive with the life that the New Testament writers so often speak about. He is alive in the sense that he has never been put to death as a result of confrontation with the law." (Morris)

ii. "He was quite secure amid all his sin and sinfulness. He lived in the sense that the deathblow had not yet killed him. He sat secure in the house of his ignorance like a man living on a volcano and thought that all was well." (Lenski)

b. **But when the commandment came, sin revived and I died**: When we do come to know the law, the law shows us our guilt and it excites our rebellion, bringing forth more sin and death.

5. (10-12) Sin corrupts the law and defeats its purpose of giving life; once law is corrupted by sin, it brings death.

And the commandment, which *was* to *bring* life, I found to *bring* death. For sin, taking occasion by the commandment, deceived me, and by it killed *me*. Therefore the law *is* holy, and the commandment holy and just and good.

a. **And the commandment, which was to bring life, I found to bring death**: Sin does this by *deception*. Sin deceives us:

- Because sin falsely promises satisfaction
- Because sin falsely claims an adequate excuse
- Because sin falsely promises an escape from punishment

b. **For sin . . . deceived me**: It isn't the law that deceives us, but it is sin that uses the law as an occasion for rebellion. This is why Jesus said, *you shall know the truth, and the truth will set you free* (John 8:32). The truth makes us free from the deceptions of sin.

c. **And by it killed me**: Sin, when followed, leads to death - not life. One of Satan's greatest deceptions is to get us to think of sin as something *good* that an unpleasant God wants to deprive us of. When God warns us away from sin, He warns us away from something that will *kill* us.

d. **Therefore the law is holy**: Paul understands how someone might take him as saying that he is against the law - but he isn't at all. It is true that we must die to sin (Romans 6:2) and we must die to the law (Romans 7:4). But that should not be taken to mean that Paul believes that sin and law are in the same basket. The problem is in us, not in the law. Nevertheless, sin corrupts the work or effect of the law, so we must die to both.

C. The purpose and character of the law.

1. (13) The law exposes and magnifies sin.

Has then what is good become death to me? Certainly not! But sin, that it might appear sin, was producing death in me through what is good, so that sin through the commandment might become exceedingly sinful.

a. **Sin, that it might appear sin, was producing death in me through what is good**: Though the law provokes our sin nature, this can be used for good because it more dramatically exposes our deep sinfulness. After all, if sin can use something as good as the law to its advantage in promoting evil, it shows how evil sin is.

> i. We need **sin** to **appear sin**, because it always wants to hide in us and conceal its true depths and strength. "This is one of the most deplorable results of sin. It injures us most by taking from us the capacity to know how much we are injured. It undermines the man's constitution, and yet leads him to boast of unfailing health; it beggars him, and tells him he is rich; it strips him, and makes him glory in his fancied robes." (Spurgeon)

> ii. "The *law*, therefore, is the grand instrument in the hands of a faithful minister, to alarm and awaken sinners." (Clarke)

b. **So that sin through the commandment might become exceedingly sinful**: Sin "becomes more sinful" in light of the law in two ways. First, sin becomes **exceedingly sinful** in contrast to the law. Second, sin becomes **exceedingly sinful** because the law provokes its evil nature.

> i. "Instead of being a dynamo that gives us power to overcome, the Law is a magnet that draws out of us all kinds of sin and corruption." (Wiersbe)

> ii. **Exceedingly sinful**: "Why didn't he say, 'exceedingly black,' or 'exceedingly horrible,' or 'exceedingly deadly'? Why, because there is nothing in the world so bad as sin. When he wanted to use the very worst word he could find to call sin by, he called it by its own name, and reiterated it: 'sin,' 'exceedingly sinful.' " (Spurgeon)

2. (14) The spiritual law cannot restrain a carnal man.

For we know that the law is spiritual, but I am carnal, sold under sin.

a. **But I am carnal**: The word **carnal** simply means "of the flesh." Paul recognizes that a **spiritual** law cannot help a **carnal** man.

> i. **Carnal** uses the ancient Greek word *sarkikos*, which means, "characterized by the flesh." In this context it speaks of the person who can and should do differently but does not. Paul sees this carnality in himself, and knows that the **law**, though it **is spiritual**, has no answer for his **carnal** nature.

b. **Sold under sin**: Paul is in bondage **under sin** and the **law** can't help him out. He is like a man arrested for a crime and thrown in jail. The law will only help him if he is innocent, but Paul knows that he is guilty and that the law argues *against* him, not *for* him.

c. Even though Paul says that he is **carnal**, it doesn't mean that he is not a Christian. His *awareness* of carnality shows that God did a work in him.

i. Luther on **but I am carnal, sold under sin**: "That is the proof of the spiritual and wise man. He knows that he is carnal, and he is displeased with himself; indeed, he hates himself and praises the Law of God, which he recognizes because he is spiritual. But the proof of a foolish, carnal man is this, that he regards himself as spiritual and is pleased with himself."

D. The struggle of obedience in our own strength.

1. (15-19) Paul describes his sense of helplessness.

For what I am doing, I do not understand. For what I will to do, that I do not practice; but what I hate, that I do. If, then, I do what I will not to do, I agree with the law that *it is* good. But now, *it is* no longer I who do it, but sin that dwells in me. For I know that in me (that is, in my flesh) nothing good dwells; for to will is present with me, but *how* to perform what is good I do not find. For the good that I will *to do,* I do not do; but the evil I will not *to do,* that I practice.

a. **For what I am doing, I do not understand**: Paul's problem isn't a lack of desire - he *wants* to do what is right (**what I will to do, that I do not practice**). His problem isn't knowledge - he *knows* what the right thing is. His problem is a lack of *power*: **how to perform what is good I do not find**. He lacks power because the law gives no power.

i. The law says: "Here are the rules and you had better keep them." But it gives us no power for keeping the law.

b. **It is no longer I who do it, but sin that dwells in me**: Is Paul denying his responsibility as a sinner? No. He recognizes that as he sins, he acts *against* his nature as a new man in Jesus Christ. A Christian must own up to his sin, yet realize that the impulse to sin does not come from who we really are in Jesus Christ.

i. "To be saved from sin, a man must at the same time own it and disown it; it is this practical paradox which is reflected in this verse. A true saint may say it in a moment of passion, but a sinner had better not make it a principle." (Wuest)

2. (20-23) The battle between two selves.

Now if I do what I will not *to do,* it is no longer I who do it, but sin that dwells in me. I find then a law, that evil is present with me, the one who wills to do good. For I delight in the law of God according to the inward man. But I see another law in my members, warring against the law of my mind, and bringing me into captivity to the law of sin which is in my members.

a. **I find then a law, that evil is present with me**: Anyone who has tried to do good is aware of this struggle. We never know how hard it is to stop sinning until we try. "No man knows how bad he is until he has tried to be good." (C.S. Lewis)

b. **For I delight in the law of God according to the inward man**: Paul knows that his real **inward man** has a **delight in the law of God**. He understands that the impulse towards sin comes from **another law in my members**. Paul knows that the "real self" is the one who does **delight in the law of God**.

> i. The old man is not the real Paul; the old man is dead. The flesh is not the real Paul; the flesh is destined to pass away and be resurrected. The *new man is the real Paul*; now Paul's challenge is to live like God has made him.

> ii. There is a debate among Christians as to if Paul was a Christian during the experience he describes. Some look at his struggle with sin and believe that it must have been before he was born again. Others believe that he is just a Christian struggling with sin. In a sense this is an irrelevant question, for this is the struggle of anyone who tries to obey God in their own strength. This experience of struggle and defeat is something that a Christian *may* experience, but something that a non-Christian *can only* experience.

> iii. Morris quoting Griffith Thomas: "The one point of the passages is that it describes a man who is trying to be good and holy by his own efforts and is beaten back every time by the power of indwelling sin; it thus refers to anyone, regenerate or unregenerate."

c. **Warring against the law of my mind, and bringing me into captivity to the law of sin**: Sin is able to war within Paul and win because there is no power in himself other *than* himself, to stop sinning. Paul is caught in the desperate powerlessness of trying to battle sin in the power of *self*.

E. The victory found in Jesus Christ.

1. (24) Paul's desperation and perspective.

O wretched man that I am! Who will deliver me from this body of death?

a. **O wretched man that I am!** The ancient Greek word **wretched** is more literally, "wretched through the exhaustion of hard labor." Paul is completely worn out and wretched because of his unsuccessful effort to please God under the principle of Law.

> i. "It is worth bearing in mind that the great saints through the ages do not commonly say, 'How good I am!' Rather, they are apt to bewail their sinfulness." (Morris)

ii. Legalism always brings a person face to face with their own wretchedness, and if they continue in legalism, they will react in one of two ways. Either they will deny their wretchedness and become self-righteous Pharisees, or they will despair because of their wretchedness and give up following after God.

b. **O wretched man that I am!** The entire tone of the statement shows that Paul is *desperate* for deliverance. He is overwhelmed with a sense of his own powerlessness and sinfulness. We must come to the same place of desperation to find victory.

i. Your desire must go beyond a vague hope to be better. You must cry out *against yourself* and cry out *unto God* with the desperation Paul had.

c. **Who will deliver me**: Paul's perspective finally turns to something (actually, *someone*) outside of himself. Paul has referred to *himself* some 40 times since Romans 7:13. In the pit of his unsuccessful struggle against sin, Paul became entirely self-focused and self-obsessed. This is the place of any believer living under law, who looks to self and personal performance rather than looking first to Jesus.

i. The words "**Who will deliver me**" show that Paul has given up on himself, and asks "**Who will deliver me?**" instead of "How will I deliver myself?"

ii. "It is not the voice of one desponding or doubting, but of one breathing and panting after deliverance." (Poole)

d. **Who will deliver me from this body of death?** When Paul describes **this body of death**, some commentators see a reference to ancient kings who tormented their prisoners by shackling them to decomposing corpses. Paul longed to be free from the wretched **body of death** clinging to him.

i. "It was the custom of ancient tyrants, when they wished to put men to the most fearful punishments, to tie a dead body to them, placing the two back to back; and there was the living man, with a dead body closely strapped to him, rotting, putrid, corrupting, and this he must drag with him wherever he went. Now, this is just what the Christian has to do. He has within him the new life; he has a living and undying principle, which the Holy Spirit has put within him, but he feels that everyday he has to drag about with him this dead body, this body of death, a thing as loathsome, as hideous, as abominable to his new life, as a dead stinking carcass would be to a living man." (Spurgeon)

ii. Others see a reference to sin in general, such as Murray: "*Body* has been taken to means *mass* and body of death *the whole mass of sin.* Hence what Paul longs to be delivered from is sin in all its aspects and consequences."

iii. "By the *body of death* he means the whole mass of sin, or those ingredients of which the whole man is composed; except that in him there remained only relics, by the captive bonds of which he was held." (Calvin)

2. (25) Paul finally looks outside of himself to Jesus.

I thank God; through Jesus Christ our Lord! So then, with the mind I myself serve the law of God, but with the flesh the law of sin.

a. **I thank God; through Jesus Christ our Lord!** Finally, Paul looks outside of himself and unto Jesus. As soon as he looks to Jesus, he has something to **thank God** for - and he thanks God **through Jesus Christ our Lord**.

i. **Through** means that Paul sees Jesus standing between himself and God, bridging the gap and providing the way to God. **Lord** means Paul has put Jesus in the right place - as **Lord** and master of his life.

b. **So then, with the mind I myself serve the law of God, but with the flesh the law of sin**: He acknowledges the state of struggle, but thanks God for the victory in Jesus. Paul doesn't pretend that looking to Jesus takes away the struggle - Jesus works **through** us, not *instead* of us in the battle against sin.

i. The glorious truth remains: there *is* victory in Jesus! Jesus didn't come and die just to give us more or better rules, but to live out His victory through those who believe. The message of the gospel is that there is victory over sin, hate, death, and all evil as we surrender our lives to Jesus and let Him live out victory through us.

c. **Through Jesus Christ our Lord**: Paul shows that even though the law is glorious and good, it can't save us - and we need a Savior. Paul never found any peace, any praising God until he looked outside of himself and beyond the law to his Savior, Jesus Christ.

i. You thought the problem was that you didn't *know what to do* to save yourself - but the law came as a teacher, taught you what to do and you *still* couldn't do it. You don't need a teacher, you need a *Savior*.

ii. You thought the problem was that you weren't *motivated* enough, but the law came in like a coach to encourage you on to do what you need to do and you still didn't do it. You don't need a coach or a motivational speaker, you need a *Savior*.

iii. You thought the problem was that you *didn't know yourself* well enough. But the law came in like a doctor and perfectly diagnosed your sin problem but the law couldn't heal you. You don't need a doctor, you need a *Savior*.

Romans 8 - A New and Wonderful Life in the Spirit

A. Life in the Spirit contrasted with life in the flesh.

1. (1) No condemnation.

There is therefore now no condemnation to those who are in Christ Jesus, who do not walk according to the flesh, but according to the Spirit.

a. **There is therefore now no condemnation**: The simple declaration of **no condemnation** comes to those who are **in Christ Jesus**. Since God the Father does not condemn Jesus, neither can the Father condemn those who are **in** Jesus. They *are* not condemned, they *will* not be condemned, and they *cannot* be condemned.

i. Paul's **therefore** is important. It means that what he says comes from a logical argument. It's as if Paul begins, "I can prove what I say here." This is what he proves: if we are one with Jesus and He is our head, we can't be condemned. You can't acquit the head and condemn the hand. You can't drown the foot as long as the head is out of water. Joined to Him, we hear the verdict: "**no condemnation**."

ii. **In Christ**: "This phrase imports, that there is a mystical and spiritual union betwixt Christ and believers. This is sometimes expressed by Christ being in them . . . and here by their being in Christ. Christ is in believers by His Spirit, and believers are in Christ by faith." (Poole)

iii. The verdict is *not* "less condemnation." That's where many believe they are - thinking our standing has *improved* in Jesus. It has not been improved, it's been completely transformed, changed to a satus of **no condemnation**.

iv. We perhaps need to consider the flip side: If you are *not* in Jesus Christ, *there is condemnation for you.* "It is no pleasant task to us to have to speak of this matter; but who are we that we should ask for pleasant tasks? What God hath witnessed in Scripture is the sum and substance of what the Lord's servants are to testify to the people. If you are not in Christ Jesus, and are walking after the flesh, you have not escaped from condemnation." (Spurgeon)

b. **No condemnation**: This place of confidence and peace comes after the confusion and conflict that marked Romans 7. Now Paul looks to Jesus and he finds his standing in Him. But this chapter is more than just the answer to Romans 7; it ties together thoughts from the very beginning of the letter.

i. Romans 8 begins with **no condemnation**; it ends with *no separation*, and in between there is *no defeat*.

c. **Who do not walk according to the flesh, but according to the Spirit**: These words are not found in the earliest ancient manuscripts of the Book of Romans and they do not agree with the flow of Paul's context here. They were probably added by a copyist who either made a mistake or thought he could "help" Paul by adding these words from Romans 8:4.

i. While it is true that those who are **in Christ** *should* not and *do* not consistently **walk according to the flesh, but according to the Spirit**, this is not a *condition* for their status of **no condemnation**. Our position in Jesus Christ is the reason for our standing of **no condemnation**.

ii. "The most learned men assure us that it is no part of the original text. I cannot just now go into the reasons for this conclusion, but they are very good and solid. The oldest copies are without it, the versions do not sustain it, and the fathers who quoted abundance of Scripture do not quote this sentence." (Spurgeon)

d. **No condemnation**: We receive this glorious declaration from God's court. We receive it though we certainly *deserve* condemnation. We receive this standing because Jesus bore the condemnation we deserved and our identity is now in Him. As He is condemned no more, neither are we.

2. (2-4) The contrast between life in the Spirit and life in the flesh.

For the law of the Spirit of life in Christ Jesus has made me free from the law of sin and death. For what the law could not do in that it was weak through the flesh, God *did* by sending His own Son in the likeness of sinful flesh, on account of sin: He condemned sin in the flesh, that the righteous requirement of the law might be fulfilled in us who do not walk according to the flesh but according to the Spirit.

a. **The law of the Spirit of life in Christ Jesus has made me free from the law of sin and death**: The **law of the sin and death** was a strong and seemingly absolute law. Every sin we commit and every cemetery we see proves it. But **the law of the Spirit of life in Christ** is stronger still, and **the law of the Spirit** frees us from **the law of sin and death**.

> i. We are free from the **law of sin**. Though he inevitably does, the Christian does not *have* to sin, because he is freed from sin's dominion. We are free from the law of **death**; death therefore no longer has any lasting power against the believer.

> ii. Romans 8:1 tells us we are free from the *guilt* of sin. Romans 8:2 tells us we are free from the *power* of sin.

b. **For what the law could not do in that it was weak through the flesh**: The **law** can do many things. It can guide us, teach us, and tell us about God's character. But the **law** cannot give energy to our **flesh**; it can give us the standard, but it can't give us the power to please God.

> i. Morris, quoting Manson: "Moses' law has right but not might; sin's law has might but not right; the law of the Spirit has both right and might."

> ii. "The law is weak to us, because we are weak to it: the sun cannot give light to blind eye, not from any impotency in itself, but merely from the incapacity of the subject it shines upon." (Poole)

c. **In that it was weak through the flesh**: The law is weak because it speaks to our **flesh**. It comes to fleshly men and speaks to them as fleshly men. But the work of the Spirit transforms us by the crucifixion of the old man and it imparts the new man - a principle higher than the flesh.

> i. "A vine does not produce grapes by Act of Parliament; they are the fruit of the vine's own life; so the conduct which conforms to the standard of the Kingdom is not produced by any demand, not even God's, but is the fruit of that divine nature which God gives as the result of what he has done in and by Christ." (Hooke)

d. **What the law could not do in that it was weak through the flesh, God did by sending His own Son**: The law could not *defeat* sin; it could only *detect* sin. Only Jesus can *defeat* sin, and He did just that through His work on the cross.

e. **By sending His own Son in the likeness of sinful flesh**: In order to defeat sin, Jesus had to identify with those bound by it, by coming **in the likeness of sinful flesh**. Under the inspiration of the Holy Spirit, Paul carefully chose his words here, indicating that Jesus was not sinful flesh, but He identified with it entirely.

> i. We could not say that Jesus came *in sinful flesh*, because He was sinless. We could not say that Jesus came *in the likeness of flesh*, because He really was human, not just *like* a human. But we can say that Jesus

came **in the likeness of sinful flesh** because although He was human, He was not sinful in Himself.

ii. **He condemned sin in the flesh**: Sin was **condemned** in the **flesh** of Jesus as He bore the condemnation we deserved. Since we are *in Christ*, the condemnation we deserve passes us over.

f. **That the righteous requirement of the law might be fulfilled in us**: Because Jesus fulfilled the **righteous requirement of the law**, and because we are in Christ, we fulfill the law. The law is fulfilled in us in regard to *obedience*, because Jesus' righteousness stands for ours. The law is fulfilled in us in regard to *punishment*, because any punishment demanded by the law was poured out upon Jesus.

i. Paul does not say that *we* fulfill the **righteous requirement of the law**. He carefully says that the righteous requirement of the law is **fulfilled in us**. It isn't fulfilled *by* us, but **in us**.

ii. Simply put, Jesus is our substitute. Jesus was treated as a sinner so we can be treated as righteous.

g. **In us who do not walk according to the flesh but according to the Spirit**: The people who enjoy this are those **who do not walk according to the flesh but according to the Spirit**. Their life is marked by obedience to the Holy Spirit, not by obedience to the flesh.

i. God wants the Spirit to rule over our flesh. When we allow the flesh to reign over the Spirit, we find ourselves bound by the sinful patterns and desperation that marked Paul's life in his "Romans 7" struggle. Our **walk** - the pattern of our life - must be **according to the Spirit**, not **according to the flesh**.

ii. Walking **in the Spirit** means that the course, the direction, the progress of one's life is directed by the Holy Spirit. It is continued and progressive motion.

iii. "Observe carefully that the flesh is there: he does not walk after it, but it is there. It is there, striving and warring, vexing and grieving, and it will be there till he is taken up into heaven. It is there as an alien and detested force, and not there so as to have dominion over him. He does not walk after it, nor practically obey it. He does not accept it as his guide, nor allow it to drive him into rebellion." (Spurgeon)

3. (5-8) The futility of trying to please God in the flesh.

For those who live according to the flesh set their minds on the things of the flesh, but those *who live* according to the Spirit, the things of the Spirit. For to be carnally minded *is* death, but to be spiritually minded *is* life and peace. Because the carnal mind *is* enmity against God; for it

is not subject to the law of God, nor indeed can be. So then, those who are in the flesh cannot please God.

a. **Set their minds on the things of the flesh**: Paul gives an easy way for us to determine if we walk in the Spirit or walk in the flesh - to simply see where our *mind* is **set**. The mind is the strategic battleground where the flesh and the Spirit fight.

> i. We shouldn't think those who **set their minds on the things of the flesh** are only notorious sinners. They may be noble people who have good intentions. Peter meant well when he told Jesus to avoid the cross, but Jesus responded to Peter with these strong words: *you are not mindful of the things of God, but the things of men* (Matthew 16:23).

b. **For to be carnally minded is death**: When our minds are set on the things of the flesh (**carnally minded**) we bring **death** into our lives. But walking in the Spirit brings **life and peace**.

> i. We must, however, guard against a false spirituality and see that Paul means the flesh insofar as it is an instrument in our rebellion against God. Paul is not talking about normal physical and emotional needs we may think about, only the sinful gratification of those needs.

c. **Because the carnal mind is enmity against God**: The flesh battles against God because it does not want to be crucified and surrendered to the Lord Jesus Christ. It does not want to live out Galatians 5:24: *those who are Christ's have crucified the flesh with its passions and desires.* In this battle to tame the flesh, the law is powerless.

> i. Paul didn't say that the carnal mind was *at* enmity with God - he put it even stronger than that. **The carnal mind is enmity against God**. "It is not black, but blackness; it is not *at* enmity, but *enmity* itself; it is not corrupt, but corruption; it is not rebellious, it is rebellion; it is not wicked, it is wickedness itself. The heart, though it be deceitful, is positively deceit; it is evil in the concrete, sin in the essence, it is the distillation, the quintessence of all things that are vile; it is not envious against God, it is envy; it is not at enmity, it is actual enmity." (Spurgeon)

d. **It is not subject to the law of God, nor indeed can be**: We can try to do good in life without being **subject to the law of God**. We may hope to put God "in debt" to us by good works, thinking God owes us. But it doesn't work. **In the flesh we cannot please God**, even if the flesh does religious things that are admired by men.

> i. Newell on Romans 8:7: "Perhaps no one text of Scripture more completely sets forth the hideously lost state of man after the flesh."

4. (9-11) Christians are empowered to live in the Spirit.

But you are not in the flesh but in the Spirit, if indeed the Spirit of God dwells in you. Now if anyone does not have the Spirit of Christ, he is not His. And if Christ *is* in you, the body *is* dead because of sin, but the Spirit *is* life because of righteousness. But if the Spirit of Him who raised Jesus from the dead dwells in you, He who raised Christ from the dead will also give life to your mortal bodies through His Spirit who dwells in you.

a. **But you are not in the flesh but in the Spirit if indeed the Spirit of God dwells in you**: Because the Holy Spirit is given to each believer when they are born again, every Christian has within themselves a principle higher and more powerful than the flesh.

i. "Many sincere people are yet spiritually under John the Baptist's ministry of repentance. Their state is practically that of the struggle of Romans Seven, where neither Christ nor the Holy Spirit is mentioned, but only a quickened but undelivered soul in struggle under a sense of 'duty,' not a sense of full acceptance in Christ and sealing by the Holy Spirit." (Newell)

b. **Now if anyone does not have the Spirit of Christ, he is not His**: This means every believer has the Holy Spirit. It is a misnomer to divide Christians among the "Spirit-filled" and the "non-Spirit-filled." If a person is not filled with the Holy Spirit, they are not a Christian at all.

i. However, many do miss out on living the Christian life in the constant fullness of the Spirit because they are not *constantly being filled with the Holy Spirit* as Paul commanded in Ephesians 5:18. They have no experience of what Jesus spoke about when He described *rivers of living water* flowing from the believer (John 7:37-39).

ii. How does one know that they have the Spirit? Ask these questions:

- Has the Spirit led you to Jesus?
- Has the Spirit put in you the desire to honor Jesus?
- Is the Spirit leading you to be more like Jesus?
- Is the Spirit at work in your heart?

c. **And if the Spirit of Christ is in you, the body is dead because of sin**: Because Jesus lives in us, the old man (**body**) is dead, but the Spirit lives and reigns, and will live out His salvation even through our mortal bodies through resurrection.

i. Not only are we *in Christ* (Romans 8:1), but He also **is in you**, and because God cannot abide a sinful home, the **body** (old man) had to die when Jesus came in.

B. Our obligation: to live in the Spirit.

1. (12-13) Our debt is to the Spirit, not to the flesh.

Therefore, brethren, we are debtors; not to the flesh, to live according to the flesh. For if you live according to the flesh you will die; but if by the Spirit you put to death the deeds of the body, you will live.

a. **We are debtors – to the flesh, to live according to the flesh**: The **flesh** (again, in the narrow sense of sinful flesh in rebellion against God) gave us nothing good. So we have no obligation to oblige or pamper it. Our debt is to the Lord, not to **the flesh**.

b. **For if you live according to the flesh you will die**: Paul constantly reminds us that living after the flesh ends in *death*. We need the reminder because we are often deceived into thinking that the flesh offers us *life*.

c. **By the Spirit you put to death the deeds of the body**: When we **put to death the deeds of the body** (force the sinful flesh to submit to the Spirit), we must do it **by the Spirit**. Otherwise we will become like the Pharisees and spiritually proud.

i. Paul tells us that not only are we saved by the work of the Spirit, but we also must walk by the Spirit if we want to grow and pursue holiness in the Lord. We cannot be like some among the Galatians who thought they could *begin* in the Spirit but then find spiritual perfection through the flesh (Galatians 3:3).

2. (14-15) Living in the Spirit means living as a child of God.

For as many as are led by the Spirit of God, these are sons of God. For you did not receive the spirit of bondage again to fear, but you received the Spirit of adoption by whom we cry out, "Abba, Father."

a. **These are the sons of God**: It is only fitting that the **sons of God** should be **led by the Spirit of God**. However, we should not think that being **led by the Spirit** is a pre-condition to being a son of God. Instead, we become sons first and then the Spirit of God leads us.

i. Paul didn't say, "As many as go to church, these are the sons of God." He didn't say, "As many as read their Bibles, these are the sons of God." He didn't say, "As many as are patriotic Americans, these are the sons of God." He didn't say, "As many as take communion, these are the sons of God." In this text, the test for sonship is whether or not a person is **led by the Spirit of God**.

ii. How does the Holy Spirit lead us?

- We are led by *guidance*
- We are led by *drawing*
- We are led by *governing authority*

- We are led as we *cooperate with* the leading. "It does not say, 'As many as are driven by the Spirit of God.' No, the devil is a driver, and when he enters either into men or into hogs he drives them furiously. Remember how the whole herd ran violently down a steep place into the sea. Whenever you see a man fanatical and wild, whatever spirit is in him it is not the Spirit of Christ." (Spurgeon)

iii. Where does the Holy Spirit lead us?

- He leads us to *repentance*
- He leads us to think *little of self* and *much of Jesus*
- He leads us into *truth*
- He leads us into *love*
- He leads us into *holiness*
- He leads us into *usefulness*

b. **For you did not receive the spirit of bondage again to fear, but you received the Spirit of adoption**: Living as a child of God means an intimate, joyful relationship with God, not like the **bondage** and **fear** demonstrated by the law. A child of God can have a relationship with God so close that they may cry out, **Abba, Father!** (Daddy!)

c. **We cry out, "Abba, Father."** It is easy for us to think of Jesus relating to the Father with this joyful confidence, but we may think we are disqualified for it. However, remember that we are *in Christ* - we have the privilege of relating to the Father even as Jesus Christ does.

i. "In the Roman world of the first century AD an adopted son was a son deliberately chosen by his adoptive father to perpetuate his name and inherit his estate; he was no whit inferior in status to a son born in the ordinary course of nature." (Bruce)

ii. Under Roman adoption, the life and standing of the adopted child changed completely. The adopted son lost all rights in his old family and gained all new rights in his new family; the old life of the adopted son was completely wiped out, with all debts being canceled, with nothing from his past counting against him any more.

3. (16) The evidence we are children of God: the testimony of the Holy Spirit.

The Spirit Himself bears witness with our spirit that we are children of God,

a. **The Spirit Himself bears witness to our spirit that we are children of God**: Plainly put, Paul says that those who are God's children, born again by the Spirit of God, *know* their status because the Holy Spirit testifies to our spirit that this is so.

i. This is not to say that there are not those who wrongly *think* or *assume* they are God's children apart from the Spirit's testimony. There are also Christians whose heads are so foggy from spiritual attack that they begin to believe the lie that they are not God's children after all. Nevertheless the **witness** of the **Spirit** is still there.

b. **We are children of God**: We don't have to wonder if we are really Christians or not. God's **children** know who they are.

i. Jewish law stated that at the mouth of two or three witnesses everything had to be established (Deuteronomy 17:6). There are two witnesses to our salvation: our own witness and the witness of the Spirit.

4. (17) The benefits and responsibilities of being God's children.

And if children, then heirs; heirs of God and joint heirs with Christ, if indeed we suffer with *Him*, that we may also be glorified together.

a. **And if children, then heirs**: Because we are *in Christ*, we have the privilege of relating to the Father as Jesus does. Therefore, we are **heirs of God and joint heirs with Christ**.

i. Being a child of God also means having an inheritance. In Luke 18:18 the rich young ruler asked Jesus, "*what must I do to inherit?*" But the rich young ruler missed the point because inheritance is not a matter of doing, it is a matter of *being* - of *being* in the right family.

b. **If indeed we suffer with Him**: Because we are *in Christ*, we are also called to share in His suffering. God's children are not immune from trials and suffering.

c. **If indeed we suffer with Him, that we may also be glorified together**: In fact, our sharing in present suffering is a *condition* of our future glorification. As far as God is concerned, it is all part of the same package of sonship, no matter how much our flesh may want to have the inheritance and the glory *without* the suffering.

C. Life in the Spirit makes us able to understand and endure suffering.

1. (18) Paul's analysis of the present suffering and our future glory: they cannot be compared to each other.

For I consider that the sufferings of this present time are not worthy *to be compared* with the glory which shall be revealed in us.

a. **For I consider that the sufferings of this present time are not worthy to be compared**: Paul was not *ignorant* or *blind* to the sufferings of human existence; he experienced more of them than most any of us today. Yet he still considered that the future glory far outweighed the present **sufferings**.

b. **The glory which shall be revealed in us**: Without a heavenly hope, Paul considered the Christian life foolish and tragic (1 Corinthians 15:19). Yet in light of eternity it is the wisest and best choice anyone can make.

c. **Revealed in us**: This coming glory will not only be revealed *to* us, but it will actually be **revealed in us**.

i. God has put this glory into the believer *right now*. In heaven the glory will simply be **revealed**. "The glory will be *revealed*, not created. The implication is that it is already existent, but not apparent." (Morris)

2. (19-22) All of creation is awaiting and anticipating this coming glory.

For the earnest expectation of the creation eagerly waits for the revealing of the sons of God. For the creation was subjected to futility, not willingly, but because of Him who subjected *it* in hope; because the creation itself also will be delivered from the bondage of corruption into the glorious liberty of the children of God. For we know that the whole creation groans and labors with birth pangs together until now.

a. **The earnest expectation of the creation eagerly waits**: Paul considers that creation itself is eagerly awaiting the **revealing of the sons of God**. This is because the creation was **subjected to futility** on account of man's sin, and will benefit from the ultimate redemption of men.

i. Isaiah 11:6-9 describes this redemption of creation in that day: *The wolf also shall dwell with the lamb, the leopard shall lie down with the young goat, the calf and the young lion and the fatling together; and a little child shall lead them. The cow and the bear shall graze; their young ones shall lie down together; and the lion shall eat straw like the ox. The nursing child shall play by the cobra's hole, and the weaned child shall put his hand in the viper's den. They shall not hurt nor destroy in all My holy mountain, for the earth shall be full of the knowledge of the LORD as the waters cover the sea.*

b. **Him who subjected it in hope**: Only God could subject creation **in hope**. This was not ultimately the work of either man or Satan.

c. **The glorious liberty of the children of God**: This benefits not only the children of God themselves, but also all of creation. Until that day, creation **groans and labors with birth pangs**.

d. **The revealing of the sons of God**: Certain groups with a "super-Christian" mentality take the idea of the **revealing of the sons of God** to say that all creation is waiting for their particular group of super-spiritual Christians to be revealed in an incredibly powerful fashion. This is a purely egotistical fantasy.

e. **The whole creation groans and labors with birth pangs together until now**: "Creation is not undergoing death pangs . . . but birth pangs." (Morris)

3. (23-25) We also groan and wait with perseverance for the coming glory.

Not only *that*, but we also who have the firstfruits of the Spirit, even we ourselves groan within ourselves, eagerly waiting for the adoption, the redemption of our body. For we were saved in this hope, but hope that is seen is not hope; for why does one still hope for what he sees? But if we hope for what we do not see, we eagerly wait for *it* with perseverance.

  a. **Who have the firstfruits of the Spirit**: This means we have a taste of the glory to come. Can we be faulted if we long for the *fulfillment* of what we have received in the **firstfruits**?

  b. **Eagerly waiting for the adoption**: We are waiting for our **adoption**. Although there is a sense in which we are already adopted (Romans 8:15), there is also a sense in which we wait for the consummation of our adoption which will happen at **the redemption of our body**.

    i. God does not ignore our physical bodies in His plan of redemption. His plan for these bodies is *resurrection*, when *this corruptible must put on incorruption, and this mortal must put on immortality* (1 Corinthians 15:53).

  c. **We eagerly wait for it with perseverance**: The fulfillment of our redemption is something still distant, yet we **hope** for it in faith and **perseverance**, trusting that God is faithful to His word and the promised glory will be a reality.

    i. Morris on **perseverance**: "It is the attitude of the soldier who in the thick of battle is not dismayed but fights on stoutly whatever the difficulties."

4. (26-27) God's help through the Spirit is available to us now.

Likewise the Spirit also helps in our weaknesses. For we do not know what we should pray for as we ought, but the Spirit Himself makes intercession for us with groanings which cannot be uttered. Now He who searches the hearts knows what the mind of the Spirit *is,* because He makes intercession for the saints according to *the will of* God.

  a. **Likewise the Spirit also helps in our weaknesses**: When we are weak, and do not know exactly how we should pray, God Himself (through the Holy Spirit) helps by making intercession for us.

  b. **Groanings which cannot be uttered**: This help from the Spirit may include praying with the spiritual gift of tongues (1 Corinthians 14:2, 14-15), but it is certainly not *limited* to praying in an unknown tongue.

    i. The idea is simply of communication beyond our ability to express. The deep **groanings** within us cannot be articulated apart from the interceding work of the Holy Spirit.

ii. This, of course, is the *purpose* of the gift of tongues - to enable us to communicate with God in a manner that is not limited to our own knowledge or ability to articulate our heart before God. The purpose of tongues *is not* to prove that we are "filled with the Spirit" or to prove that we are especially spiritual.

c. **According to the will of God**: The Holy Spirit's help in intercession is perfect because He **searches the hearts** of those whom He helps, and He is able to guide our prayers **according to the will of God**.

5. (28-30) God's help is an enduring promise; He has the ability to work all things for good and to see us through to glorification.

And we know that all things work together for good to those who love God, to those who are the called according to *His* purpose. For whom He foreknew, He also predestined *to be* conformed to the image of His Son, that He might be the firstborn among many brethren. Moreover whom He predestined, these He also called; whom He called, these He also justified; and whom He justified, these He also glorified.

a. **And we know that all things work together for good**: God's sovereignty and ability to manage every aspect of our lives is demonstrated in the fact that **all things work together for good to those who love God**, though we must face *the sufferings of this present time* (Romans 8:18). God is able to make even those sufferings work together for our good and His good.

b. **All things**: God is able to work **all things**, not some things. He works them for good **together**, not in isolation. This promise is for those **who love God** in the Biblical understanding of love, and God manages the affairs of our life because we are **called according to His purpose**.

c. **For whom He foreknew, He also predestined to be conformed to the image of His Son**: The eternal chain of God's working is seen in the connection between **foreknew**, **predestined**, **called**, **justified**, and **glorified**. God didn't begin a work in the Romans simply to abandon them in the midst of their present suffering.

i. "Paul is saying that God is the author of our salvation, and that from beginning to end. We are not to think that God can take action only when we graciously give him permission." (Morris)

ii. "Of course I believe in predestination, since it's plainly taught in the Scriptures. The doctrine could be assumed, even if the word was never explicitly used. It's a thrilling truth that doesn't upset me at all. The fact that He chose me and began a good work in me proves that He'll continue to perform it. He wouldn't bring me this far and then dump me." (Smith)

d. **To be conformed to the image of His Son**: However, our participation in this eternal plan is essential, reflected in its goal: that we might be **conformed to the image of His Son**; and this is a process that God does with our cooperation, not something He just "does" to us.

e. **That He might be the firstborn among many brethren**: This is the *reason* for God's plan. He adopts us into His family (Romans 8:15) for the purpose of making us like Jesus Christ, similar to Him in the perfection of His humanity.

D. The triumphant victory of the life in the Spirit.

1. (31) Paul begins his conclusion to this section: **If God be for us, who can be against us?**

What then shall we say to these things? If God *is* for us, who *can be* against us?

a. **If God is for us, who can be against us?** If all we had were the first few chapters of the Book of Romans, some might believe that God was *against* us. Now that Paul has shown the lengths that God went to save man from His wrath and equip him for victory over sin and death, who can doubt that God is **for us**?

i. "Our weak hearts, prone to legalism and unbelief, receive these words with great difficulty: *God is for us*...They have failed Him; but He is *for* them. They are ignorant; but He is *for* them. They have not yet brought forth much fruit; but He is *for* them." (Newell)

ii. Most all men say or think that God is for them - terrorists commit horrible crimes thinking that God is for them. Nevertheless, the Holy Spirit guards this statement with an "**if**," so we may know that just because a man *thinks* God is with him does not make it so. God is only **for us** if we are reconciled to Him through Jesus Christ.

b. **Who can be against us?** Likewise, despite the suffering Christians face, if God is for them, what does it matter if others are against them? One person plus God makes an unconquerable majority.

i. We certainly can be deceived into thinking that **God is for us** when He actually is not (as do cultists and those like them). Yet it cannot be denied that for those who are in Jesus Christ, God is **for** them!

2. (32) Evidence that God is for us: the gift of Jesus Christ.

He who did not spare His own Son, but delivered Him up for us all, how shall He not with Him also freely give us all things?

a. **He who did not spare His own Son**: If the Father already gave His ultimate gift, how can we think that He won't give us the smaller gifts?

3. (33-39) The security of the believer in God's love.

Who shall bring a charge against God's elect? *It is* **God who justifies. Who** *is* **he who condemns?** *It is* **Christ who died, and furthermore is also risen, who is even at the right hand of God, who also makes intercession for us. Who shall separate us from the love of Christ?** *Shall* **tribulation, or distress, or persecution, or famine, or nakedness, or peril, or sword? As it is written: "For Your sake we are killed all day long; we are accounted as sheep for the slaughter." Yet in all these things we are more than conquerors through Him who loved us. For I am persuaded that neither death nor life, nor angels nor principalities nor powers, nor things present nor things to come, nor height nor depth, nor any other created thing, shall be able to separate us from the love of God which is in Christ Jesus our Lord.**

a. **Who shall bring a charge against God's elect?** We are secure from every charge against us. If we are declared "not guilty" by the highest Judge, who can bring an additional charge?

b. **Who is he who condemns?** We are secure from all condemnation. If Jesus is our advocate, promoting our benefit, then who can condemn us?

c. **More than conquerors through Him who loved us**: No matter what our circumstances, none of the **sufferings of this present time** can separate us from the love of God. This makes us **conquerors** and more.

i. Earle on **nakedness**: "This term today suggests indecency on parade. Then it meant a lack of clothes simply because one had no ways or means of getting any."

ii. **Sword**: This word implies execution. It is the only item on the list that Paul had not yet personally experienced (1 Corinthians 4:11, 15:30).

d. **More than conquerors**: How is the Christian *more* than a conqueror?

- He overcomes with a greater *power*, the power of Jesus
- He overcomes with a greater *motive*, the glory of Jesus
- He overcomes with a greater *victory*, losing nothing even in the battle
- He overcomes with a greater *love*, conquering enemies with love and converting persecutors with patience

e. **Nor any other created thing, shall be able to separate us from the love of God which is in Christ Jesus our Lord**: Nothing which appears to be good or nothing which appears to be evil can **separate us from the love of God**.

Romans 9 - Has God Rejected Israel?

A. Paul's heart for Israel.

1. Chapter 9 brings a slight shift in focus to the Book of Romans.

a. In Romans chapters one through eight, Paul thoroughly convinced us about man's need and God's glorious provision in Jesus Christ through the Holy Spirit.

b. Now, in Romans 9 through 11, Paul deals with the problem associated with the condition of Israel. What does it mean that Israel has missed its Messiah? What does this say about God? What does it say about Israel? What does it say about *our* present position in God?

i. The question goes something like this: How can I be secure in God's love and salvation to me when it seems that Israel was once loved and saved, but now seems to be rejected and cursed? Will God also reject and curse me one day?

ii. "If God cannot bring his ancient people into salvation, how do Christians know that he can save them? Paul is not here proceeding to a new and unrelated subject. These three chapters are part of the way he makes plain how God in fact saves people." (Morris)

2. (1-2) Paul's sorrow.

I tell the truth in Christ, I am not lying, my conscience also bearing me witness in the Holy Spirit, that I have great sorrow and continual grief in my heart.

a. **I have great sorrow and continual grief in my heart**: In Romans 8 Paul left us at the summit of glory, assuring us that nothing can *separate us from the loved of God which is in Christ Jesus our Lord*. So why has Paul now become so somber in his tone?

b. **Sorrow and continual grief**: Paul feels this because he considers a people who seem to be separated from God's love - unbelieving Israel, who rejected God's Messiah.

c. **I tell the truth in Christ, I am not lying, my conscience also bearing me witness in the Holy Spirit**: Paul uses every possible assurance to declare his great sorrow over Israel. This is something that really bothered Paul and was on his heart.

3. (3-5) The source of Paul's sorrow.

For I could wish that I myself were accursed from Christ for my brethren, my countrymen according to the flesh, who are Israelites, to whom *pertain* **the adoption, the glory, the covenants, the giving of the law, the service** *of God,* **and the promises; of whom** *are* **the fathers and from whom, according to the flesh, Christ** *came,* **who is over all,** *the* **eternally blessed God. Amen.**

a. **I could wish that I myself were accursed from Christ for my brethren**: This is a dramatic declaration of Paul's great love and sorrow for his brethren. Paul says he himself is willing to be separated from Jesus if that could somehow accomplish the salvation of Israel.

i. We should not think that Paul merely uses a dramatic metaphor here. The solemn assurances he gave in Romans 9:1 remind us he is being completely truthful.

ii. This great passion for souls gave Paul perspective. Lesser things did not trouble him because he was troubled by a great thing - the souls of men. "Get love for the souls of men - then you will not be whining about a dead dog, or a sick cat, or about the crotchets of a family, and the little disturbances that John and Mary may make by their idle talk. You will be delivered from petty worries (I need not further describe them) if you are concerned about the souls of men . . . Get your soul full of a great grief, and your little griefs will be driven out." (Spurgeon)

b. **I could wish that I myself were accursed**: Paul reflects the same heart Moses had in Exodus 32:31-32: *Then Moses returned to the LORD and said, "Oh, these people have committed a great sin, and have made for themselves a god of gold! Yet now, if You will forgive their sin; but if not, I pray, blot me out of Your book which You have written."*

i. Of course Paul also shows the heart of Jesus, who was cursed on behalf of others that they might be saved (Galatians 3:13).

ii. We should remember that when it came to ministry, the Jews were Paul's worst enemies. They harassed and persecuted him from town to town, stirring up lies and violence against him. Yet he still loved them this passionately.

iii. "It is not easy to estimate the measure of love in a Moses and a Paul. For our limited reason does not grasp it, as the child cannot comprehend the courage of warriors!" (Bengel)

c. **The adoption, the glory, the covenants, the giving of the law, the services of God, and the promises**: The pain Paul feels for his lost brethren is all the more severe when he considers how God has blessed them with all the privileges of being His own special people.

i. **The glory** speaks of God's Shekinah glory, the visible "cloud of glory" showing God's presence among His people.

d. **Of whom are the fathers and from whom, according to the flesh, Christ came**: Paul also considers the human legacy of being God's chosen people. Israel not only gave us the great **fathers** of the Old Testament, but Jesus Himself came from Israel. This entire spiritual legacy makes Israel's unbelief all the more problematic.

e. **Christ . . . who is over all, the eternally blessed God, Amen**: This is one of Paul's clear statements that Jesus is God. Those who prefer a punctuation that says otherwise impose their preconceived views on the text. "The grammatical arguments almost all favor the first position [that it says that Christ is God], but most recent scholars accept the second [that God here refers to the Father] on the grounds that Paul nowhere else says explicitly that Christ is God." (Morris)

i. Wuest, quoting Robertson: "[This is a] clear statement of the deity of Christ following the remark about His humanity. This is the natural and obvious way of punctuating the sentence. To make a full stop after *flesh* and start a new sentence for the doxology is very abrupt and awkward."

B. Why Israel is in its present condition from God's perspective: Israel missed the Messiah because it was according to God's sovereign plan.

1. (6-9) Has God failed with His plan regarding Israel? No; God has not failed His children of promise.

But it is not that the word of God has taken no effect. For they *are* not all Israel who *are* of Israel, nor *are they* all children because they are the seed of Abraham; but, "In Isaac your seed shall be called." That is, those who *are* the children of the flesh, these *are* not the children of God; but the children of the promise are counted as the seed. For this *is* the word of promise: "At this time I will come and Sarah shall have a son."

a. **It is not that the word of God has taken no effect**: Paul thinks of someone looking at Israel and saying, "God's word didn't come through for them. He didn't fulfill His promise for them because they missed their Messiah and now seem cursed. How do I know that He will come through for me?" Paul answers the question by asserting that **it is not that the word of God has taken no effect**.

b. **For they are not all Israel who are of Israel**: One meaning of the name **Israel** is "governed by God." Paul says here that not all **Israel** is really "governed by God." Did God's word fail? No; instead, **they are not all** *governed by God* **who are of Israel**.

> i. "Paul tells us that no one is truly Israel unless he is governed by God. We have a parallel situation with the word 'Christian.' Not everyone who is called a Christian is truly a follower of Christ." (Smith)

c. **The children of the promise are counted as the seed**: God's word didn't fail, because God still reaches His **children of the promise**, which may or may not be the same as physical Israel.

> i. Paul shows that merely being the descendant of Abraham saves no one. For example, Ishmael was just as much a son of Abraham as Isaac was; but Ishmael was a son according to the flesh, and Isaac was a son according to the promise (**At this time I will come and Sarah will have a son**). One was the heir of God's covenant of salvation, and one was not. Isaac stands for the **children of the promise** and Ishmael stands for the **children of the flesh**.

2. (10-13) Another example of the fact that promise is more important than natural relation: Jacob and Esau.

And not only *this,* **but when Rebecca also had conceived by one man,** *even* **by our father Isaac (for** *the children* **not yet being born, nor having done any good or evil, that the purpose of God according to election might stand, not of works but of Him who calls), it was said to her, "The older shall serve the younger." As it is written, "Jacob I have loved, but Esau I have hated."**

a. **Our father Isaac**: God's choice between Ishmael and Isaac seems somewhat logical to us. It's a lot harder to understand why God chose Jacob to be the heir of God's covenant of salvation instead of Esau. We might not understand it as easily, but God's choice is just as valid.

b. **Not yet being born, nor having done any good or evil**: Paul points out that God's choice was not based on the performance of Jacob or Esau. The choice was made before they were born.

c. **That the purpose of God according to election might stand, not of works but of Him who calls**: So we do not think that God chose Jacob over Esau because He knew their works in advance, Paul points out that it was **not of works**. Instead, the reason for choosing was found in **Him who calls**.

d. **The older shall serve the younger**: God announced these intentions to Rebecca before the children were born, and He repeated His verdict long after Jacob and Esau had both passed from the earth (**Jacob I have loved, but Esau I have hated**).

> i. We should regard the **love** and the **hate** as regarding His purpose in choosing one to become the heir of the covenant of Abraham. In that regard, God's preference could rightly be regarded as a display of **love** towards Jacob and **hate** towards Esau.

> ii. Morris cites examples where **hate** clearly seems to mean something like "loved less" (Genesis 29:31, 33; Deuteronomy 21:15; Matthew 6:24; Luke 14:26; John 12:25). Yet he agrees with Calvin's idea that the real thought here is much more like "accepted" and "rejected" more than our understanding of the terms "loved" and "hated."

> iii. All in all, we see that Esau *was* a blessed man (Genesis 33:8-16, Genesis 36). God *hated* Esau in regard to inheriting the covenant, not in regard to blessing in this life or the next.

> iv. "A woman once said to Mr. Spurgeon, 'I cannot understand why God should say that He hated Esau.' 'That,' Spurgeon replied, 'is not my difficulty, madam. My trouble is to understand how God could love Jacob.' " (Newell)

> v. Our greatest error in considering the choices of God is to think that God chooses for arbitrary reasons, as if He chooses in an "eeny-meeny-miny-moe" way. We may not be able to fathom God's reasons for choosing, and they are reasons He alone knows and answers to, but God's choices are *not* capricious. He has a plan and a reason.

3. (14-16) Does God's choice of one over another make God unrighteous?

What shall we say then? *Is there* **unrighteousness with God? Certainly not! For He says to Moses, "I will have mercy on whomever I will have mercy, and I will have compassion on whomever I will have compassion." So then** *it is* **not of him who wills, nor of him who runs, but of God who shows mercy.**

> a. **Is there unrighteousness with God?** Paul answers this question strongly: **Certainly not!** God clearly explains His right to give mercy to whomever He pleases in Exodus 33:19.

> b. **I will have mercy on whomever I will have mercy**: Remember what **mercy** is. Mercy is *not* getting what we do deserve. God is never *less* than fair with anyone, but fully reserves the right to be *more* than fair with individuals as He chooses.

> > i. Jesus spoke of this right of God in the parable of the landowner in Matthew 20:1-16.

ii. We are in a dangerous place when we regard God's mercy towards us as our *right*. If God is obliged to show mercy, then it is not mercy - it is obligation. No one is ever *unfair* for *not* giving mercy.

c. **So then it is not of him who wills, nor of him who runs, but of God who shows mercy**: God's mercy is not given to us because of what we wish to do (**him who wills**), or because of what we actually do (**him who runs**), but simply out of His desire to show mercy.

4. (17-18) The example of Pharaoh.

For the Scripture says to Pharaoh, "For this very purpose I have raised you up, that I may show My power in you, and that My name may be declared in all the earth." Therefore He has mercy on whom He wills, and whom He wills He hardens.

a. **For this very purpose I have raised you up**: God allowed Pharaoh in the days of Moses to rise to power so that God could show the strength of His judgment against Pharaoh, and thereby glorify Himself.

b. **Therefore He has mercy on whom He wills, and whom He wills He hardens**: Sometimes God will glorify Himself through showing mercy; sometimes God will glorify Himself through a man's hardness.

i. We should not think that God persuaded an unwilling, kind-hearted Pharaoh to be hard towards God and Israel. In hardening the heart of Pharaoh, God simply allowed Pharaoh's heart to pursue its natural inclination.

c. **He hardens**: We know that Pharaoh did harden his own heart, according to Exodus 7:13, 7:22, 8:15, 8:19, 8:32, 9:7, and 9:34. But "He does not so much as bother to indicate that Pharaoh hardened his own heart, an evidence of unbelief and rebellion, because he is emphasizing the freedom of God's action in all cases." (Harrison)

5. (19-21) Does God's right to choose relieve man of responsibility?

You will say to me then, "Why does He still find fault? For who has resisted His will?" But indeed, O man, who are you to reply against God? Will the thing formed say to him who formed *it*, "Why have you made me like this?" Does not the potter have power over the clay, from the same lump to make one vessel for honor and another for dishonor?

a. **You will say to me then, "Why does He still find fault? For who has resisted His will?"** Paul imagines someone asking, "If it is all a matter of God's choice, then how can God find fault with me? How can anyone go against God's choice?"

b. **Indeed, O man, who are you to reply against God?** Paul replies by showing how disrespectful such a question is. If God says He chooses, and if God also says that we are responsible before Him, who are we to question Him?

c. **Does not the potter have power over the clay**: Does not God have the same right that any Creator has over his creation? Therefore, if God declares that we have an eternal responsibility before Him, then it is so.

6. (22-24) Doesn't God have the right to glorify Himself as He sees fit?

What **if God, wanting to show** *His* **wrath and to make His power known, endured with much longsuffering the vessels of wrath prepared for destruction, and that He might make known the riches of His glory on the vessels of mercy, which He had prepared beforehand for glory,** *even* **us whom He called, not of the Jews only, but also of the Gentiles?**

a. **What if God**: Again, the same principle from God's dealing with Pharaoh is repeated. If God chooses to glorify Himself through letting people go their own way and letting them righteously receive His wrath so as to **make His power known**, who can oppose Him?

b. **He might make known the riches of His glory on the vessels of mercy**: As well, if God desires to be *more* than fair with others, showing them His mercy, who can oppose Him?

c. **But also of the Gentiles**: And if God wants to show mercy to the Gentiles as well as the Jews (of course, never being *less* than fair to either), who can oppose Him?

i. "The Jews were inclined to think that God could not make them anything other than vessels of honor. Paul rejects this view and points out that God does what he wills." (Morris)

d. **Vessels of wrath prepared for destruction**: Paul does not say that *God* has prepared them for destruction. Those vessels do an adequate job on their own.

7. (25-26) The prophet Hosea (in Hosea 2:23 and 1:10) declares God's right to choose, calling those who previously were not called His people.

As He says also in Hosea: "I will call them My people, who were not My people, and her beloved, who was not beloved." And it shall come to pass in the place where it was said to them, 'You *are* **not My people,' there they shall be called sons of the living God."**

a. **You are not My people**: These passages from Hosea 2:23 and 1:10 show the mercy of God. God told the prophet Hosea to name one of his children *Lo-Ammi*, meaning "Not My People." Yet God also promised that this judgment would not last forever. One day Israel will be restored and once again be called **sons of the living God**.

8. (27-29) Isaiah (in Isaiah 10:23 and 1:9) declares God's right to choose a remnant among Israel for salvation.

Isaiah also cries out concerning Israel: "Though the number of the children of Israel be as the sand of the sea, the remnant will be saved. For He will finish the work and cut *it* short in righteousness, because the Lord will make a short work upon the earth." And as Isaiah said before: "Unless the Lord of Sabaoth had left us a seed, we would have become like Sodom, and we would have been made like Gomorrah."

a. **The remnant will be saved**: The passage quoted from Isaiah 10:23 speaks first to God's work in saving a remnant from the coming Assyrian destruction. The suffering of God's people at the hands of the Assyrians and others would make them feel as if they would certainly be destroyed. God assures them that this is not the case. He will always preserve His **remnant**.

i. God has always dealt with a **remnant**. "It was stupid to think that, since the whole nation had not entered the blessing, the promise of God had failed. The promise had not been made to the whole nation and had never been intended to apply to the whole nation." (Morris)

b. **We would have become like Sodom**: Sodom and Gomorrah were *completely* destroyed in judgment. This quotation from Isaiah 1:9 shows that as bad as Judah's state was because of their sin, it could have been worse. It was only by the mercy of God that they survived at all. **Sodom** and **Gomorrah** were both totally destroyed, with not even a **very small remnant** to carry on. Even in the midst of judgment, God showed His mercy to Judah.

i. The merciful promise is clear: "But if *only* a remnant will survive, *at least* a remnant will survive, and constitute the hope of restoration." (Bruce)

C. Why Israel is in its present condition from man's perspective: Israel missed the Messiah because they refuse to come by faith.

1. (30-31) Analyzing the present situation of Israel and the Gentiles according to a human perspective.

What shall we say then? That Gentiles, who did not pursue righteousness, have attained to righteousness, even the righteousness of faith; but Israel, pursuing the law of righteousness, has not attained to the law of righteousness.

a. **Gentiles, who did not pursue righteousness, have attained to righteousness**: By all appearances the Gentiles found righteousness even though it did not seem that they really looked for it.

b. **But Israel . . . has not attained to the law of righteousness**: By all appearances Israel seemed to work for the righteousness of God with everything it had, but did not find it.

c. **Attained to righteousness . . . not attained**: What was the difference? Why did the unlikely Gentiles find righteousness, when the likely Jews did not? Because the Gentiles pursued **the righteousness of faith**, and the Jews pursued **the law of righteousness**. The Gentiles who were saved came to God through faith, receiving His righteousness. The Jews who seem to be cast off from God tried to justify themselves before God by performing works according to **the law of righteousness**.

2. (32-33) Paul emphasizes the reason why Israel seems cast off from God's goodness and righteousness: **Because they did not seek it by faith**.

Why? Because *they did* not *seek it* by faith, but as it were, by the works of the law. For they stumbled at that stumbling stone. As it is written: "Behold, I lay in Zion a stumbling stone and rock of offense, And whoever believes on Him will not be put to shame."

a. **Because they did not seek it by faith**: We might expect Paul to answer the question "**Why?**" again from God's perspective, and simply throw the matter back on God's sovereign choice. Instead, he places the responsibility with Israel: **Because they did not seek it by faith . . . they stumbled at that stumbling stone**.

i. Paul has already shown in Romans that the only possible way to be saved is through faith, not the works of the law; and that this salvation comes only through the work of a crucified Savior - which was a stumbling block to Israel (1 Corinthians 1:22-23).

b. **For they stumbled at that stumbling stone**: Paul shows that Israel is responsible for their present condition. Has he contradicted everything he has previously said, which emphasized God's sovereign plan? Of course not, he simply presents the problem from the other side of the coin - the side of human responsibility, instead of the side of God's sovereign choice.

Romans 10 - Israel's Present Rejection of God

A. Israel's rejection of the gospel of salvation through Jesus Christ.

1. (1-3) Israel's refusal to submit to the righteousness of God.

Brethren, my heart's desire and prayer to God for Israel is that they may be saved. For I bear them witness that they have a zeal for God, but not according to knowledge. For they being ignorant of God's righteousness, and seeking to establish their own righteousness, have not submitted to the righteousness of God.

a. **Brethren, my heart's desire and prayer to God for Israel**: Paul again feels compelled to relate his **heart** regarding his fellow Jews. Paul does not rejoice that they have *stumbled at that stumbling stone* (Romans 9:32).

i. Paul's **heart's desire** also translated into concrete action: **prayer to God for Israel**. Paul didn't just "care," he prayed.

b. **I bear them witness that they have a zeal for God**: Paul will readily recognize that Israel has **a zeal for God** but he also sees that it is zeal **not according to knowledge**.

i. This is where so many religious people - even sincere Christians - go astray. They have plenty of **zeal** but little **knowledge**.

ii. **Zeal for God, but not according to knowledge**: This is a perfect description of Paul himself before his conversion. Saul of Tarsus was a notorious persecutor of Christians before Jesus confronted him on the road to Damascus (Acts 9:1-20).

iii. It's remarkable that Paul found something good to say about these Jewish people who persecuted him so mercilessly. "At least they have a **zeal for God**," Paul says.

c. **Establish their own righteousness**: This effort shows Israel's lack of **knowledge** and that they are **ignorant of God's righteousness**. Paul ably demonstrated in the first several chapters of Romans how futile this is. Plainly put, *by the deeds of the law no flesh will be justified* (Romans 3:20).

d. Seeking to establish their own righteousness, have not submitted to the righteousness of God: Israel had a lack of **knowledge**. But that wasn't their only problem. They also had a *moral* problem: they **have not submitted to the righteousness of God**.

> i. People cannot come to Jesus without the right information about the gospel, but information alone is not enough to save anyone. There must be a radical *submission* to the righteousness of God, putting away our own righteousness.

> ii. Again, we cannot neglect the emphasis on *personal responsibility*. All of Paul's teaching of God's election and right to choose does not diminish man's responsibility.

2. (4-8) The contrast between God's righteousness and our attempts at righteousness.

For Christ *is* the end of the law for righteousness to everyone who believes. For Moses writes about the righteousness which is of the law, "The man who does those things shall live by them." But the righteousness of faith speaks in this way, "Do not say in your heart, 'Who will ascend into heaven?' " (that is, to bring Christ down *from above)* or, " 'Who will descend into the abyss?' " (that is, to bring Christ up from the dead). But what does it say? "The word is near you, in your mouth and in your heart" (that is, the word of faith which we preach):

a. Christ is the end of the law: Jesus is the **end of the law** for those who believe. The law *ends* for the believer in the sense that our obedience to the law is no longer the basis for our relationship with God. The law has *not* come to an end in the sense of no longer reflecting God's standard or no longer showing us our need for a Savior.

> i. "Christ did not come to make the law milder, or to render it possible for our cracked and battered obedience to be accepted as a sort of compromise. The law is not compelled to lower its terms, as though it had originally asked too much; it is holy and just and good, and ought not to be altered in one jot or tittle, nor can it be. Our Lord gives the law all it requires, not a part, for that would be an admission that it might justly have been content with less at first." (Spurgeon)

b. The man who does those things shall live by them: The Law of Moses makes the path to righteousness through the law plain. If you want to live by the law (find life through the law), you must *do* the law - and do it completely and perfectly.

c. But the righteousness of faith: This is based on Jesus, and we don't have to "work" to get Jesus. It is not as if we have to **ascend into heaven or descend into the abyss** to gain Jesus. We believe and receive.

d. **But what does it say? "The word is near you, in your mouth and in your heart."** Instead of having to go to great lengths to *achieve* righteousness by the law, we can immediately *receive* righteousness by faith, by trusting in the word of the gospel.

3. (9-13) How God's righteousness is gained by faith.

That if you confess with your mouth the Lord Jesus and believe in your heart that God has raised Him from the dead, you will be saved. For with the heart one believes unto righteousness, and with the mouth confession is made unto salvation. For the Scripture says, "Whoever believes on Him will not be put to shame." For there is no distinction between Jew and Greek, for the same Lord over all is rich to all who call upon Him. For "whoever calls on the name of the LORD shall be saved."

a. **If you confess with your mouth the Lord Jesus and believe in your heart that God has raised Him from the dead, you will be saved**: We do not gain God's righteousness by works. Instead, we gain it by *confessing* and *believing* in the person and work of Jesus Christ.

b. **Confess with your mouth**: Confession has the idea of *agreeing with*. When we **confess . . . the Lord Jesus**, we agree with what God said about Jesus, and with what Jesus said about Himself. It means we recognize that Jesus is God, that He is the Messiah, and that His work on the cross is the only way of salvation for mankind.

i. **Confess with your mouth the Lord Jesus**: We can never forget all that it meant to say that Jesus Christ is **Lord**. "If a man called Jesus *kurios* he was ranking him with the Emperor and with God; he was giving him the supreme place in his life; he was pledging him implicit obedience and reverent worship." (Barclay)

ii. Wuest, quoting Robertson on **Jesus Christ is Lord**: "No Jew would do this who had not really trusted Christ, for *Kurios* in the LXX is used of God. No Gentile would do it who had not ceased worshipping the emperor as *Kurios*. The word *Kurios* was and is the touchstone of faith."

c. **Believe in your heart that God has raised Him from the dead**: We must also believe this. Some wonder why Paul didn't mention the crucifixion in this passage. But when Paul emphasizes the need to believe **that God has raised him from the dead**, it is not that we believe the resurrection as *opposed* to the cross, but *encompassing* the work of Jesus on the cross.

d. **Believe in your heart**: Mere intellectual agreement with the facts of the cross and the resurrection is not enough. You must **believe in your heart**; and even that belief is not enough without accompanying action: **confess with your mouth**.

i. "We believe everything which the Lord Jesus has taught, but we must go a step further, and trust him. It is not even enough to believe in him, as being the Son of God, and the anointed of the Lord; but we must believe on him . . . The faith that saves is not believing certain truths, nor even believing that Jesus is a Savior; but it is resting on him, depending on him, lying with all your weight on Christ as the foundation of your hope. Believe that he can save you; believe that he will save you; at any rate leave the whole matter of your salvation with him in unquestioning confidence. Depend upon him without fear as to your present and eternal salvation. This is the faith which saves the soul." (Spurgeon)

e. **For with the heart one believes unto righteousness, and with the mouth confession is made unto salvation**: These two together (belief and confession) result in **righteousness** and **salvation**. We should not ignore how scandalously simple this is (**whoever calls upon the name of the LORD shall be saved**) and what an affront this is to every attempt of the flesh to be justified or any attempt to find salvation based on national or ethnic foundation.

i. Both Jew and Greek were quick to give some credit to national or ethnic origin, as if being saved were a matter of being born into the right family. But Paul makes it clear: **There is no distinction between Jew and Greek, for the same Lord over all is rich to all who call upon Him**.

f. **The Scripture says**: "Referring, I think, to the general sense of Scripture, rather than to any one passage. There are several texts from which it may be gathered that believers shall not be put to shame." (Spurgeon)

g. **All who call upon Him**: Again, note the emphasis on *human responsibility*. From Romans 9 alone we might think that salvation is God's doing alone, but from Romans 10 we might think that salvation is man's doing alone - together we see the matter from each perspective.

4. (14-15) The necessity of the preaching of the gospel.

How then shall they call on Him in whom they have not believed? And how shall they believe in Him of whom they have not heard? And how shall they hear without a preacher? And how shall they preach unless they are sent? As it is written: "How beautiful are the feet of those who preach the gospel of peace, Who bring glad tidings of good things!"

a. **How shall they hear without a preacher? And how shall they preach unless they are sent?** Paul rightly observes that it all goes back to the preaching of the gospel, and preachers must be **sent** - both by God and the Christian community at large.

b. **How shall they hear without a preacher?** Conceivably, God could have chosen any means for the message of salvation to come, such as angelic messengers or directly working without a human preacher. Nevertheless God's "normal" way of bringing people to Jesus Christ is through the preaching of the gospel.

c. **How beautiful are the feet**: No wonder those who preach have **beautiful feet** - they partner with God for the salvation of men. The **feet** speak of activity, motion, and progress, and those who are active and moving in the work of preaching the gospel have **beautiful feet**.

d. **Glad tidings of good things**: Obviously, the salvation Isaiah prophesied about could not be salvation through works or the law. To say "You can be right before God if you work hard enough" is not a gospel of **peace**, and that message does not bring **glad tidings of good things**.

B. The prophets foretold this rejection of the gospel by Israel.

1. (16-17) The testimony of Isaiah 53:10.

But they have not all obeyed the gospel. For Isaiah says, "Lord, who has believed our report?" So then faith *comes* by hearing, and hearing by the word of God.

a. **But they have not all obeyed the gospel**: If salvation is so simple, available to all who trust in the person and work of Jesus, then why does Israel seem to be cast off from God? Because many among them had not **believed** his **report** - because they did not trust in God's word through Isaiah and other messengers of the gospel. Therefore they are not saved.

b. **So then faith comes by hearing, and hearing by the word of God**: Saving faith comes through **hearing by the word of God**. Though Israel heard, they did not exercise saving faith in Christ - making them (and us) all the more responsible.

i. "*Hearing* is a reflection of first-century life. Paul does not raise the possibility of the message being read. While there were people who could read, the ordinary first-century citizen depended rather on being able to hear something." (Morris)

2. (18) The testimony of Psalm 19:4.

But I say, have they not heard? Yes indeed: "Their sound has gone out to all the earth, and their words to the ends of the world."

a. **Their sound has gone out to all the earth**: This quotation from Psaul 19:4 proves that the word of the gospel went forth and Israel heard it. This makes them more accountable for their rejection of the good news.

i. "This might seem an exaggeration: the gospel had not been carried throughout all the earth, not even to all the lands that were known to the inhabitants of the Graeco-Roman world. Paul was well aware of that; at this very time he was planning the evangelization of Spain, a province where the name of Christ was not yet known (*c.f.* 15:18-24). But by now the gospel had been carried to most parts of the Mediterranean area where Jews were to be found; and that is all the argument requires." (Bruce)

b. **To the ends of the world**: "There is not a part of the promised land in which these glad tidings have not been preached; and there is scarcely a place in the Roman empire in which the doctrine of Christ crucified has not been heard: if, therefore, the Jews have not believed, the fault is entirely their own; as God has amply furnished them with the means of faith of salvation." (Clarke)

3. (19) The testimony of Deuteronomy 32:21.

But I say, did Israel not know? First Moses says: "I will provoke you to jealousy by *those who are* **not a nation, I will move you to anger by a foolish nation."**

a. **I will provoke you to jealousy**: God told Israel that He would bring others close to Him and make them jealous. Yet Israel ignored this word also, making them more accountable.

4. (20) The testmony of Isaiah 65:1.

But Isaiah is very bold and says: "I was found by those who did not seek Me; I was made manifest to those who did not ask for Me."

a. **Isaiah is very bold**: Isaiah's bold prophecy was a warning that Israel ignored, making them more accountable.

b. **I was found by those who did not seek Me**: It is strange that Israel, for the most part, rejected their own Messiah. Strange as it was, this too was foretold. It didn't surprise God or His prophets.

5. (21) The testimony of Isaiah 65:2.

But to Israel he says: "All day long I have stretched out My hands to a disobedient and contrary people."

a. **A disobedient and contrary people**: This tells God's assessment of disobedient, Messiah-rejecting Israel. They are a **disobedient and contrary people,** and all the more so because of their great responsibility before God.

Romans 11 - The Restoration of Israel

A. Israel and the remnant of grace.

1. (1a) Has God **cast away** (rejected) **His people** Israel?

I say then, has God cast away His people? Certainly not!

a. **Has God cast away His people?** Paul's question makes sense at this point in Romans. If Israel's rejection of the gospel was somehow both consistent with God's eternal plan (Romans 9:1-29) and Israel's own choosing (Romans 9:30-10:21), then does this mean that Israel's fate is settled, and there is no possibility of restoration?

b. **Certainly not!** Despite their present state, Israel is **not** permanently **cast away**. Now Paul will explain this answer.

2. (1b) Evidence that God has not *cast away His people*: Paul himself.

For I also am an Israelite, of the seed of Abraham, *of* the tribe of Benjamin.

a. **I also am an Israelite**: Paul's faith in Jesus as the Messiah proved there were some Jews chosen by God who embraced the gospel.

b. **I also**: Whenever we want evidence of God's work, we could and should look to our own life first. This is what Paul did and what we should do.

3. (2-5) The principle of a remnant.

God has not cast away His people whom He foreknew. Or do you not know what the Scripture says of Elijah, how he pleads with God against Israel, saying, "Lord, they have killed Your prophets and torn down Your altars, and I alone am left, and they seek my life"? But what does the divine response say to him? "I have reserved for Myself seven thousand men who have not bowed the knee to Baal." Even so then, at this present time there is a remnant according to the election of grace.

a. **God has not cast away His people whom He foreknew . . . at this present time there is a remnant**: In Paul's day Israel as a group generally rejected their Messiah. Yet a substantial remnant embraces the gospel of Jesus Christ, and God has often worked in Israel through a faithful remnant (as He did in the time of Elijah).

> i. "It is just possible that Paul, likewise persecuted by his own countrymen, felt a special kinship with Elijah." (Harrison)

b. **He pleads with God against Israel**: Things were so bad that Elijah prayed **against** his own people!

c. **LORD, they have killed Your prophets**: Elijah thought that God had cast off the nation and he was the only one left serving the Lord. But God showed him that there was in fact a substantial remnant - though it was only a remnant, it was actually there.

d. **At this present time there is a remnant**: We often think that God needs a lot of people to do a great work, but He often works through a small group, or through a group that starts out small. Though not many Jews in Paul's day embraced Jesus as Messiah, **a remnant** did and God will use that small group in a big way.

> i. "It was not the number as much as the permanence of God's plan for Israel that mattered in the time of Elijah . . . He put his trust in God's grace, not in numbers." (Morris)

4. (6-10) God's right to choose a remnant according to grace.

And if by grace, then *it is* no longer of works; otherwise grace is no longer grace. But if *it is* of works, it is no longer grace; otherwise work is no longer work. What then? Israel has not obtained what it seeks; but the elect have obtained it, and the rest were blinded. Just as it is written: "God has given them a spirit of stupor, eyes that they should not see and ears that they should not hear, to this very day." And David says: "Let their table become a snare and a trap, a stumbling block and a recompense to them. Let their eyes be darkened, so that they do not see, and bow down their back always."

a. **If by grace, then it is no longer of works, otherwise grace is no longer grace**: Paul left the previous verse noting that the remnant was chosen *according to the election of grace*. Now he reminds us what **grace** is by definition: the free gift of God, not given with an eye to performance or potential in the one receiving, but given only out of kindness in the giver.

b. **If it is of works, it is no longer grace**: As principles, grace and works don't go together. If giving is of grace, it cannot be of works, and if it is of works, it cannot be of grace.

c. **The elect have obtained it, and the rest were hardened**: The elect among Israel received and responded to the mercy of God but the rest were hardened by their rejection.

d. **Just as it is written**: The quotations from Isaiah 29 and Psalm 69 tell us that God can give a **spirit of stupor** and **eyes that they should not see** and He can say **let their eyes be darkened** as He pleases. If God is pleased to enlighten only a remnant of Israel at the present time, He may do so as He pleases.

i. Morris calls **a spirit of stupor** "an attitude of deadness towards spiritual things."

ii. "The idea is that men are sitting feasting comfortably at their banquet; and their very sense of safety has become their ruin. They are so secure in the fancied safety that the enemy can come upon them unaware" (Barclay). The Jews of Paul's day were so secure in their idea of being the chosen people that the very idea became the thing that ruined them.

B. God's plan in saving only a remnant at the present time.

1. (11a) Does Israel's stumbling as predicted by Psalm 69 mean that they have fallen away permanently?

I say then, have they stumbled that they should fall?

a. **Stumbled . . . fall**: As Paul presents it here, there is a difference between *stumbling* and *falling*. Israel **stumbled**, but they would not **fall** - in the sense of being removed from God's purpose and plan. You can recover from a stumble, but if you fall you're down.

2. (11b-14) No, God had a specific purpose to fulfill in allowing Israel to stumble - so that salvation would come to the Gentiles.

Certainly not! But through their fall, to provoke them to jealousy, salvation *has come* to the Gentiles. Now if their fall *is* riches for the world, and their failure riches for the Gentiles, how much more their fullness! For I speak to you Gentiles; inasmuch as I am an apostle to the Gentiles, I magnify my ministry, if by any means I may provoke to jealousy *those who are* my flesh and save some of them.

a. **Certainly not!** Paul has shown that God is still working through a remnant of Israel today, but wants to make it clear that the sinning majority of Israel is not lost forever.

b. **Through their fall . . . salvation has come to the Gentiles**: We should not forget that in many instances the gospel only went out to the Gentiles after the Jewish people rejected it (Acts 13:46, 18:5-6, 28:25-28). In this sense, the rejection of the gospel by the Jews was **riches for the Gentiles**.

i. It wasn't that the Jewish rejection of Jesus as Messiah *caused* Gentiles to be saved. It merely gave more opportunity for the gospel to go to the Gentiles, and many Gentiles took advantage of this opportunity.

c. **If by any means I may provoke to jealousy**: Yet, Paul's desire isn't only that these riches would be enjoyed by the Gentiles only, but that the Jews would be provoked to a good kind of **jealousy**, motivating them to receive some of the blessings the Gentiles enjoyed.

> i. "It is a matter for profound regret that just as Israel refused to accept this salvation when it was offered to them, so the Gentiles have all too often refused to *make Israel envious*. Instead of showing to God's ancient people the attractiveness of the Christian way, Christians have characteristically treated the Jews with hatred, prejudice, persecution, malice, and all uncharitableness. Christians should not take this passage calmly." (Morris)

3. (15-21) To the Gentiles: yes, Jewish rejection of Jesus was made into a blessing for you; but consider how great a blessing their acceptance of Jesus will be.

For if their being cast away *is* the reconciling of the world, what *will* their acceptance *be* but life from the dead? For if the firstfruit *is* holy, the lump *is* also *holy;* and if the root *is* holy, so *are* the branches. And if some of the branches were broken off, and you, being a wild olive tree, were grafted in among them, and with them became a partaker of the root and fatness of the olive tree, do not boast against the branches. But if you do boast, *remember that* you do not support the root, but the root supports you. You will say then, "Branches were broken off that I might be grafted in." Well *said.* Because of unbelief they were broken off, and you stand by faith. Do not be haughty, but fear. For if God did not spare the natural branches, He may not spare you either.

a. **If the firstfruit is holy**: The **firstfruit** probably represents the first Christians, who were Jewish. Their conversion was something holy and good for the church. After all, each of the apostles and most of the human authors of Scripture were Jewish. If the conversion of this **firstfruit** was good for the Gentiles, how much better will it be when the complete harvest is brought in!

> i. Many commentators take the **firstfruit** here as the patriarchs, but it fits better to see it as the original core group of Christians - who were each Jewish.

b. **Some of the branches . . . a wild olive tree**: With the picture of the tree and the branches, Paul reminds the Gentile Christians that it is only by God's grace that they can be grafted into the "tree" of God - the "root" of which is Israel.

> i. "When an old olive tree had lost its vigor, it seems that one remedy in antiquity was to cut away the failing branches and graft in some wild olive shoots. The result was said to be the invigoration of the failing tree." (Morris)

ii. The Jewish Talmud speaks of Ruth the Moabitess as a "godly shoot" engrafted into Israel. (Cited in Morris)

c. **Do not boast against the branches . . . you do not support the root, but the root supports you**: Lest Gentiles think of themselves as superior to Jews, Paul also reminds them that the root supports the branches - not the other way around.

d. **Because of unbelief they were broken off, and you stand by faith**: In addition, any Gentile standing in the "tree" of God is there by faith only, not by works or merits. If Gentiles are unbelieving, they will be "cut off" just as much as unbelieving Israel was.

4. (22-24) Application of God's purpose in Israel's rejection that the Gentiles might be reached.

Therefore consider the goodness and severity of God: on those who fell, severity; but toward you, goodness, if you continue in *His* goodness. Otherwise you also will be cut off. And they also, if they do not continue in unbelief, will be grafted in, for God is able to graft them in again. For if you were cut out of the olive tree which is wild by nature, and were grafted contrary to nature into a cultivated olive tree, how much more will these, who *are* natural *branches,* be grafted into their own olive tree?

a. **Consider the goodness and severity of God**: Paul stresses the need to **continue in His goodness**; not in the sense of a salvation by works, but continuing in God's grace and goodness to us - a relationship of continual abiding. This idea of a continual abiding in the "tree" is also expressed in John 15:1-8.

i. "The conditional clause in this verse, *if you continue in His goodness*, is a reminder that there is no security in the bond of the gospel apart from perseverance. There is no such thing as continuance in the favour of God in spite of apostasy; God's saving embrace and endurance are correlative." (Murray)

b. **God is able to graft them in again**: And, if Israel was "cut off" because of their unbelief, they can be **grafted in** again **if they do not continue in unbelief**.

i. "Evidently some Gentile believers were tempted to think that there was no future for Israel. She had rejected the gospel and it had now passed to the Gentiles; Israel was finished, rejected, cast off. God had chosen them instead. It is this kind of pride that Paul is opposing." (Morris)

c. **How much more will these, who are natural branches, be grafted into their own olive tree?** If the Gentiles seemed to "graft" into God's "tree" easily, we know it won't be hard for God to graft the **natural branches** back into the tree. We can also assume that the natural branches will have the potential to bear much fruit.

C. God's plan for Israel includes their eventual restoration.

1. (25-27) The promise that all Israel will be saved.

For I do not desire, brethren, that you should be ignorant of this mystery, lest you should be wise in your own opinion, that blindness in part has happened to Israel until the fullness of the Gentiles has come in. And so all Israel will be saved, as it is written: "The Deliverer will come out of Zion, and He will turn away ungodliness from Jacob; for this *is* My covenant with them, when I take away their sins."

a. **Lest you be wise in your own opinion**: This is a warning to take this soberly. Christians must not **be ignorant of this mystery**.

b. **Blindness in part has happened to Israel**: Paul summarizes his point from Romans 11:11-24. God's purpose in allowing **blindness in part** to come upon Israel is so that the **fullness of the Gentiles** can **come in**.

i. **In part** has the idea of "temporary"; Israel's **blindness** is temporary. "One day the Jews will realize their blindness and folly. They'll accept Jesus Christ, and the glorious national restoration of these people will bring in the Kingdom Age." (Smith)

c. **Until the fullness of the Gentiles has come in**: At that time, God will once again turn the attention of His plan of the ages specifically on Israel again, so that **all Israel will be saved**. God's plan of the ages does not set its attention on everyone equally through all ages.

d. **All Israel will be saved**: This **all Israel** is not "spiritual Israel." It isn't "spiritual Israel" in Romans 11:25, because that Israel is spiritually blind. Therefore, we shouldn't regard it as spiritual Israel in Romans 11:26.

i. There is a distinction between national or ethnic Israel and spiritual Israel. Paul makes this clear in Galatians 3:7 and other passages. Nevertheless, God still has a purpose and a plan for ethnic Israel and will bring salvation to them.

ii. We also know this is not "spiritual Israel" because Paul says this is a **mystery** - and it is no **mystery** that *spiritual* Israel will be saved.

iii. Harrison on **all Israel**: "It was the view of Calvin, for example, that the entire company of the redeemed, both Jew and Gentile, is intended. But *Israel* has not been used of Gentiles in these chapters, and it is doubtful that such is the case in any of Paul's writings."

iv. "It is impossible to entertain an exegesis which understands *Israel* here in a different sense from *Israel* in verse 25." (Bruce)

e. **Will be saved**: This states clearly for us that God is *not* finished with Israel as a nation or a distinct ethnic group. Though God has turned the focus of His saving mercies away from Israel specifically and onto the Gentiles generally, He will turn it back again.

i. This simple passage refutes those who insist that God is forever done with Israel as a people and that the Church is the New Israel and inherits every promise ever made to national and ethnic Israel of the Old Testament.

ii. We are reminded of the enduring character of the promises made to national and ethnic Israel (Genesis 13:15 and 17:7-8). God is not "finished" with Israel, and Israel is not "spiritualized" as the church.

iii. While we see and rejoice in a continuity of God's work throughout all His people through all ages, we also see a distinction between Israel and the Church - a distinction that Paul is sensitive to here.

f. **All Israel will be saved**: This does not mean there will be a time when every last person of Jewish descent will be saved. Instead, this is a time when Israel as a whole will be a saved people, and when the nation as a whole (especially its leadership) embraces Jesus Christ as Messiah.

i. Even as the apostasy of Israel did not extend to every last Jew, so the salvation of Israel will not extend to every last Jew; Paul is speaking of the "mass" of Jews when he says **all Israel**. "*All Israel* is a recurring expression in Jewish literature, where it need not mean 'every Jew without a single exception', but 'Israel as a whole.' " (Bruce)

ii. And, when **all Israel will be saved**, they will be saved through embracing Jesus Christ as Messiah - as unlikely as this seems. They are not saved with some peculiar "Jewish" salvation.

iii. The Bible indicates this is a necessary condition for the return of Jesus Christ (Matthew 23:39, Zechariah 12:10-11). Jesus will not return again until God turns the focus of His saving mercies on Israel again, and Israel responds to God through Jesus Christ.

g. **The Deliverer will come out of Zion**: The quotations from Isaiah show that God still has a redeeming work to accomplish with Israel, and that it will not be left undone.

2. (28-29) God's love and calling for Israel still endures.

Concerning the gospel *they are* enemies for your sake, but concerning the election *they are* beloved for the sake of the fathers. For the gifts and the calling of God *are* irrevocable.

a. **Concerning the gospel . . . concerning the election**: Even though it seemed that in Paul's day the Jews were enemies of God and were against

Jesus, they are still **beloved** - if for no other reason, then **for the sake of the fathers** (the patriarchs of the Old Testament).

> i. Of course, they are loved for *more* than the **sake of the fathers**, but that by itself would be enough.

b. **The gifts and the calling of God are irrevocable**: This is another reason why God hasn't given up on national and ethnic Israel. This principle, stated by Paul, comforts us far beyond its direct relevance to Israel. It means that God will not give up on us and He leaves the path open to restoration.

3. (30-32) Paul cautions the Gentile Christians to remember where they came from and where God has promised to take the Jewish people.

For as you were once disobedient to God, yet have now obtained mercy through their disobedience, even so these also have now been disobedient, that through the mercy shown you they also may obtain mercy. For God has committed them all to disobedience, that He might have mercy on all.

a. **You were once disobedient to God**: The Gentile Christians came from **disobedience**; yet God showed them mercy, in part through the disobedience of Israel.

b. **Obtained mercy through their disobedience**: If God used the disobedience of Israel for the good of Gentiles, He can also use the mercy shown to Gentiles for the mercy of Israel.

c. **God has committed them all to disobedience**: The idea is that God has shut up both Jew and Gentile into custody as lawbreakers. God offers **mercy** to these prisoners, based on the person and work of Jesus.

4. (33-36) Praise to God for His plan and the progress of the plan.

Oh, the depth of the riches both of the wisdom and knowledge of God! How unsearchable *are* His judgments and His ways past finding out! "For who has known the mind of the LORD? Or who has become His counselor? Or who has first given to Him and it shall be repaid to him?" For of Him and through Him and to Him *are* all things, to whom *be* glory forever. Amen.

a. **Oh, the depth of the riches both of the wisdom and knowledge of God!** As Paul considers God's great plan of the ages, he breaks into spontaneous praise. Paul realizes that God's **ways** are **past finding out**, and God's wisdom and knowledge is beyond him.

> i. Who would have planned the whole scenario with Israel, the Gentiles, and the Church as God has planned it? Yet, we can see the great wisdom and compassion in His plan.

ii. "It is strange that, with such a scripture as this before their eyes, men should sit down coolly and positively write about counsels and decrees of God formed from all eternity, of which they speak with as much confidence and decision as if *they* had formed a part of the council of the Most High, and had been with him in the beginning of his ways!" (Clarke)

b. **For who has known the mind of the LORD?** The quotations from Isaiah 40:13 and Job 41:11 emphasize both God's wisdom and sovereign conduct; no one can make God their debtor.

i. **Or who has first given to Him and it shall be repaid to him?** You can try all you want - but you will never make God a debtor to you. You can't out-give God. He will never need to repay a debt to anyone.

c. **Of Him and through Him and to Him are all things**: "All these words are monosyllables. A child just learning to read could easily spell them out. But who shall exhaust their meaning?" (Meyer)

i. It is all **of Him**: This plan came from God. It wasn't man's idea. We didn't say, "I've offended God and have to find a way back to Him. Let's work on a plan to come back to God." In our spiritual indifference and death we didn't care about a plan, and even if we did care we aren't smart enough or wise enough to make one. It is all **of Him**.

ii. It is all **through Him**: Even if we had the plan, we couldn't make it happen. We couldn't free ourselves from this prison of sin and self. It could only happen **through Him**, and the great work of Jesus on our behalf is the **through Him** that brings salvation.

iii. It is all **to Him**: It's not for me, it's not for you, it's all **to Him**. It is *to the praise of the glory of His grace* (Ephesians 1:6). It's for His pleasure that we are created, and we find our fulfillment in bringing Him glory and honor.

d. **To whom be glory forever**: The fact that Paul can't figure out God makes him glorify God all the more. When we understand some of the greatness of God, we worship Him all the more passionately.

Romans 12 - Living the Christian Life

A. The foundation for Christian living.

J.B. Phillips has an outstanding and memorable translation of Romans 12:1-2:

With eyes wide open to the mercies of God, I beg you, my brothers, as an act of intelligent worship, to give Him your bodies, as a living sacrifice, consecrated to Him and acceptable by Him. Don't let the world around you squeeze you into its own mould, but let God re-mould your minds from within, so that you may prove in practice that the Plan of God for you is good, meets all His demands and moves towards the goal of true maturity.

1. (1) The living sacrifice.

I beseech you therefore, brethren, by the mercies of God, that you present your bodies a living sacrifice, holy, acceptable to God, *which is* your reasonable service.

> a. **I beseech you**: This reminds us that Paul appeals to our *will*. God calls us to make a *choice* about the way that we live for Him.

> b. **Therefore brethren**: It is Paul's pattern to begin a letter with a strong doctrinal section and follow with exhortations to Christian living. Paul begs Christians to live a certain way in light of what God did for them.

>> i. "When he uses this pattern Paul is saying that the Christian life is dependent on the great Christian doctrines." (Morris)

> c. **By the mercies of God** reminds us that we do this because of the mercy shown to us by God (described well in Romans 1-11), and that we are only *able* to offer ourselves to God as He works His mercy in us. God commanded us to do this, and He makes it possible for us to do it.

>> i. "Whereas the heathen are prone to sacrifice in order to obtain mercy, biblical faith teaches that the divine mercy provides the basis of sacrifice as the fitting response." (Harrison)

>> ii. Think of all the **mercies of God** Paul has explained to us thus far:

- Justification from the guilt and penalty of sin
- Adoption in Jesus and identification with Christ
- Placed under grace, not law
- Giving the Holy Spirit to live within
- Promise of help in all affliction
- Assurance of a standing in God's election
- Confidence of coming glory
- Confidence of no separation from the love of God
- Confidence in God's continued faithfulness

iii. In light of all this mercy - past, present, and future - Paul begs us to **present your bodies a living sacrifice**. "We must believe that these Divine mercies *have persuasive powers* over our wills." (Newell)

d. **Present your bodies**: Connected with the idea of **a living sacrifice**, this calls to mind *priestly service*. Spiritually speaking, our **bodies** are brought to God's altar.

i. It is best to see the *body* here as a reference to our entire being. Whatever we say about our spirit, soul, flesh, and mind, we know that they each live in our bodies. When we give the body to God, the soul and spirit go with it. **Present your bodies** means that God wants *you*, not just your work. You may do all kinds of work for God, but never give Him your *self*.

ii. The previous appeal to the will (**I beseech you**) means that the will is to be the master over the body. The thinking of our age says that our body must tell the will what to do; but the Bible says that our will must bring the body as a living sacrifice to God. The body is a wonderful servant, but a terrible master. Keeping it at God's altar as a living sacrifice keeps the body where it should be.

iii. An ancient Greek never thought of presenting his *body* to God. They thought the body was so unspiritual that God didn't care about it. Paul shows here that God is concerned about our bodies. 1 Corinthians 6:20 reminds us that God bought our bodies with a price.

e. **A living sacrifice**: First century people, both Jews and pagans, knew first hand what sacrifice was all about. To beg that they make themselves **a living sacrifice** was a striking image.

- The sacrifice is **living** because it is *brought alive* to the altar
- The sacrifice is **living** because it *stays alive* at the altar; it is *ongoing*

f. **Holy, acceptable to God**: When we offer our body, God intends it to be a **holy** and **acceptable** sacrifice. The standard for sacrifices made to God under the New Covenant are not any less than the standard under the Old Covenant.

i. In the Old Testament, every sacrifice had to be **holy** and **acceptable to God**

- *He shall bring a male without blemish* (Leviticus 1:10)

- *But if there is a defect in it, if it is lame or blind or has any serious defect, you shall not sacrifice it to the* LORD *your God* (Deuteronomy 15:21)

ii. The idea of *a sweet aroma to the* LORD is almost always linked to the idea of *an offering made by fire*. There is a "burning" in this matter of a living sacrifice. It also shows that Paul has in mind the *burnt offering*, in which the entire sacrifice was given to the Lord. In some sacrifices, the one offering the sacrifice and the priest shared in the some of the meal, but never in the burnt offering.

iii. The holiness we bring to the altar is a *decision* for holiness, and *yielding* to the work of holiness in our life. As we present our bodies a living sacrifice, God makes our life holy by burning away impurities.

g. **Reasonable service**: The ancient Greek word for **reasonable** (*logikos*) can also be translated "of the word" (as it is in 1 Peter 2:2). **Reasonable service** is a life of worship *according to God's Word*.

i. The sacrifice of an animal was **reasonable service**, but only for the one bringing the sacrifice - not for the sacrifice itself. Under the New Covenant we have far greater mercies, so it is **reasonable** to offer a far greater sacrifice.

2. (2) Resisting conformity to the world and embracing the transformation that comes in Jesus Christ.

And do not be conformed to this world, but be transformed by the renewing of your mind, that you may prove what *is* that good and acceptable and perfect will of God.

a. **Do not be conformed to this world**: This warns us that the "world system" - the popular culture and manner of thinking that is in rebellion against God - will try to conform us to its ungodly pattern, and that process must be resisted.

b. **But be transformed by the renewing of your mind**: This is the opposite of being **conformed to this world**. The battle ground between conforming to the world and being transformed is within the **mind** of the believer. *Christians must think differently.*

i. "I don't want to be conformed to this world. I want to be transformed. How do I do it?" **By the renewing of your mind**. The problem with many Christians is they live life based on *feelings*, or they are only concerned about *doing*.

ii. The life based on *feeling* says, "How do I feel today? How do I feel about my job? How do I feel about my wife? How do I feel about worship? How do I feel about the preacher?" *This life by feeling will never know the transforming power of God*, because it ignores the **renewing of the mind**.

iii. The life based on *doing* says, "Don't give me your theology. Just tell me what to *do*. Give me the four points for this and the seven keys for that." *This life of doing will never know the transforming power of God*, because it ignores the **renewing of the mind**.

iv. God is never against the principles of feeling and doing. He is a God of powerful and passionate feeling and He commands us to be doers. Yet feelings and doing are completely insufficient *foundations* for the Christian life. The first questions cannot be "How do I feel?" or "What do I do?" Rather, they must be "What is true here? What does God's Word say?"

c. **Transformed**: This is the ancient Greek word *metamorphoo* - describing a metamorphosis. The same word is used to describe Jesus in His transfiguration (Mark 9:2-3). This is a glorious transformation!

i. The only other place Paul uses this word for **transformed** is in 2 Corinthians 3:18: *But we all, with unveiled face, beholding as in a mirror the glory of the Lord, are being transformed into the same image from glory to glory, just as by the Spirit of the Lord.* For Paul, this transformation and renewing of our minds takes place as we behold the face of God, spending time in His glory.

d. **Prove what is that good and acceptable and perfect will of God**: As we are **transformed** on the inside, the *proof* is evident on the outside, as others can see what the **good and acceptable and perfect will of God** is through our life.

i. Paul here explains how to live out the will of God:

- Keep in mind the rich mercy of God to you - past, present, and future (*by the mercies of God*)
- As an act of intelligent worship, decide to yield your entire self to Him (*present your bodies a living sacrifice*)
- Resist conformity to the thoughts and actions of this world (**do not be conformed**)
- By focus on God's word and fellowship with Him (**be transformed by the renewing of your mind**)

ii. Then, your life will *be in the will of God*. Your life will **prove what is that good and acceptable and perfect will of God**.

iii. You may *know* what the **good and acceptable and perfect will of God** is, but you can't **prove** it in your life apart from the transforming work of the Holy Spirit.

B. Living out the spiritual gifts God has given.

1. (3) A warning to live in humility.

For I say, through the grace given to me, to everyone who is among you, not to think *of himself* more highly than he ought to think, but to think soberly, as God has dealt to each one a measure of faith.

a. **To everyone among you**: Paul will soon speak about how we should exercise spiritual gifts in the body of Christ, but a warning about humility is in order, given the inordinate pride that often arises from those who regard themselves as spiritually gifted.

i. We should remember that spiritual *giftedness* does not equal spiritual *maturity*. Just because a person has substantial spiritual gifts does not mean they are necessarily spiritually mature or a worthy example.

b. **Not to think of himself more highly than he ought to think**: Paul does not advise any kind of masochistic attitude, but rather he tells us to see the truth about ourselves. When we see ourselves as we really are, it is impossible to be given over to pride.

c. **God has dealt to each one a measure of faith**: This means that we should see even our saving faith as a gift from God, and that we have no basis for pride or a superior opinion of ourselves.

2. (4-5) Unity and diversity in the body of Christ.

For as we have many members in one body, but all the members do not have the same function, so we, *being* many, are one body in Christ, and individually members of one another.

a. **Many members in one body**: The church is a unified whole (**one body**), yet we are distinct within that one body (**individually members**). In the body of Christ there is unity but not uniformity.

b. **Individually members of one another**: We err when we neglect either aspect; unity should never be promoted at the expense of individuality, and individuality should never diminish the church's essential unity **in Christ**; *He* is our common ground, we are **one body in Christ**.

3. (6-8) An exhortation to use (and how to use) the gifts God has granted to the individual members of the church.

Having then gifts differing according to the grace that is given to us, *let us use them*: if prophecy, *let us prophesy* in proportion to our faith; or ministry, *let us use it* in *our* ministering; he who teaches, in teaching; he

who exhorts, in exhortation; he who gives, with liberality; he who leads, with diligence; he who shows mercy, with cheerfulness.

a. **Having then gifts**: The difference and distribution of gifts is all due to **the grace that is given to us**. Spiritual gifts are not given on the basis of merit, but because God chooses to give them.

i. This idea is related in the ancient Greek word for "spiritual gifts": *charismata*, which means a gift of grace. This term was apparently coined by Paul to emphasize that the giving of these spiritual gifts was all of grace.

ii. Spiritual gifts are given at the discretion of the Holy Spirit. 1 Corinthians 12:11 says, *But one and the same Spirit works all these things, distributing to each one individually as He wills.*

iii. Knowing this should be an insurmountable barrier to pride in the exercise of spiritual gifts. However man, in the depravity of his heart, finds a way to be proud about spiritual gifts and insists on exalting men for how God has gifted them.

b. **If prophecy**: **Prophecy** must be practiced **in proportion to our faith**. God may give us something to say to an individual or church body that stretches our faith. If we can't prophecy in faith and trust that God has really spoken to us, we shouldn't do it at all.

i. We are reminded that **prophecy**, in the Biblical understanding, isn't necessarily "fore-telling" in a strictly predictive sense. It is more accurately "forth-telling" the heart and mind of God, which may or may not include a predictive aspect.

ii. This warns us against flippant, "stream of consciousness" prophecy that has no difficulty saying, "Thus says the Lord" at the drop of a hat.

iii. **In proportion to our faith**: The ancient Greek text actually has "the" before **faith**. Paul may be cautioning that prophecy must be *according to the faith*, in accord with the accepted body of doctrine held among believers.

iv. Some take the **proportion** of **faith** to be the proportion of the faith of the audience of the prophecy; this has truth also.

c. **Ministry**: This has in view the broader picture of simply serving in practical ways. Paul sees this as important ministry from the Holy Spirit as well.

d. **Teaching**: This has in mind *instruction*, while **exhortation** encourages people to practice what they have been taught; both are necessary for a healthy Christian life.

i. Those who are taught but not exhorted become "fat sheep" that only take in and never live the Christian life. Those who are exhorted but not taught become excited and active, but have no depth or understanding to what they do and will burn out quickly or will work in wrong ways.

e. **He who gives**: This refers to someone who is a channel through whom God provides resources for His body. This is an important *spiritual* gift that must be exercised with **liberality**. When someone who is called and gifted to be a giver stops giving Iiberally, they will often see their resources dry up - having forgotten *why* God has blessed them.

f. **He who leads**: This one must show **diligence**. It is easy for leaders to become discouraged and feel like giving up, but they must persevere if they will please God by their leadership.

g. **He who shows mercy**: This gift needs **cheerfulness**. It can be hard enough to show mercy, but even harder to be *cheerful* about it. This reminds us that the gift of showing mercy is a supernatural gift of the Spirit.

C. A series of brief instructions on living like a Christian with others.

This section shows one thing clearly: Paul knew the teaching of Jesus, especially the Sermon on the Mount

1. (9-13) Relating to those in the Christian family.

Let love be without hypocrisy. Abhor what is evil. Cling to what is good. Be kindly affectionate to one another with brotherly love, in honor giving preference to one another; not lagging in diligence, fervent in spirit, serving the Lord; rejoicing in hope, patient in tribulation, continuing steadfastly in prayer; distributing to the needs of the saints, given to hospitality.

a. **Let love be without hypocrisy**: Of course, love *with* hypocrisy isn't real love at all; but much of what masquerades as "love" in the Christian community is laced with hypocrisy, and must be demonstrated against.

b. **Abhor what is evil. Cling to what is good**: In some ways, it is often easier for us to *either* **abhor what is evil** or **cling to what is good** rather than doing both. The godly person knows how to practice both.

c. **Be kindly affectionate to one another**: This is a command, that Christians should not have a cold, stand-offish attitude. **In honor giving preference to one another** shows that the displays of affection are genuine.

i. We should see in this, as much as anything, a call to simple *good manners* among Christians.

d. **Not lagging in diligence, fervent in spirit, serving the Lord**: If we are called to warm relations and good manners, we also know that we are called to hard work. The church is no place for laziness.

i. **Fervent in spirit** could be translated, "with respect to the spirit, boiling."

e. **Rejoicing in hope**: The call to **hope** usually has in mind our ultimate reward with Jesus. Paul says we serve God **rejoicing in hope**, not *rejoicing in results*. This shows how we are commanded to do all these things with an eye towards heaven. This how we fulfill the command for **hope**, **patience** and **steadfast** character described here.

f. **Patient in tribulation**: Difficult times do not excuse us when we abandon **hope** or **patience** or **continuing steadfastly in prayer**. Trials do not excuse a lack of love in the body of Christ or a lack of willingness to do His work.

i. Leon Morris explains these two important words. **Patient** "denotes not a passive putting up with things, but an active, steadfast endurance." **Tribulation** "denotes not some minor pinprick, but deep and serious trouble."

g. **Distributing to the needs of the saints, given to hospitality**: Our care and concern will demonstrate itself in practical deeds done for others, either going to them (**distributing to the needs of the saints**) or inviting them to come to us (**given to hospitality**)

i. The ancient Greek word for **hospitality** is literally translated "love for strangers." In addition, "**given**" is a strong word, sometimes translated "persecute" (as in Romans 12:14). The idea is to "pursue" people you don't know with hospitality. This is love in *action*, not just feelings.

2. (14) Relating to those outside of the Christian family.

Bless those who persecute you; bless and do not curse.

a. **Bless those who persecute you**: We are not to have a hateful attitude towards anyone, not even towards those who persecute us.

b. **Do not curse**: Jesus spoke of this same heart in Matthew 5:46: *For if you love those who love you, what reward have you? Do not even the tax collectors do the same?* The surpassing greatness of the love of Jesus in us is shown in that it can be extended to our enemies.

c. **Who persecute you**: Of course, not all persecution comes from outside the church. Jesus told us *the time is coming that whoever kills you will think that he offers God service* (John 16:2).

3. (15-21) How to get along with people both inside and outside the church.

Rejoice with those who rejoice, and weep with those who weep. Be of
the same mind toward one another. Do not set your mind on high things,
but associate with the humble. Do not be wise in your own opinion.
Repay no one evil for evil. Have regard for good things in the sight of
all men. If it is possible, as much as depends on you, live peaceably with
all men. Beloved, do not avenge yourselves, but *rather* give place to
wrath; for it is written, "Vengeance *is* Mine, I will repay," says the
Lord. Therefore "If your enemy is hungry, feed him; if he is thirsty,
give him a drink; for in so doing you will heap coals of fire on his head."
Do not be overcome by evil, but overcome evil with good.

a. **Rejoice with those who rejoice, and weep with those who weep**:
This is how we can fulfill the command to **be of the same mind toward
one another**. It is a simple command to be considerate of the feelings of
others instead of waiting for them to be considerate of your feelings.

b. **Associate with the humble**: Paul cautions us to have a humble mind-
set. In refusing to set our **mind on high things** and in associating **with
the humble**, we simply imitate Jesus. **Do not be wise in your own opinion** reminds us of how far we still have to go in actually being like Jesus.

c. **Repay no one evil for evil** recalls Jesus' command in Matthew 5:38-45.
We are to love our enemies and treat well those who treat us badly.

d. **Have regard for good things in the sight of all men** is a way to live
out the idea of praising what is good. People should be able to see what is
good and what is not based on our conduct.

e. **Live peaceably with all men** reminds us that though we are in contrast to the world, we do not seek out contention. **If it is possible**, we will
be at peace with all men.

i. "*If it be possible* indicates that it may not always be possible." (Murray)

f. **Do not avenge yourselves**: The one who trusts in God will not think it
necessary to **avenge** themselves. They will leave the issue of vengeance to
God, and **give place to wrath** - giving *no* place to their own wrath, and a
wide place to God's wrath.

g. **Overcome evil with good**: With this mind-set, we will do good to our
enemies, looking for the most practical ways we can help them. This is the
way we are not **overcome by evil, but overcome evil with good**.

i. Is the heaping **coals of fire on his head** something good in the
eyes of our **enemy** or is it something bad? It most likely refers to a
"burning conviction" that our kindness places on our enemy. Or, some
think it refers to the practice of lending coals from a fire to help a
neighbor start their own - an appreciated act of kindness.

Romans 13 - A Christian's Obligation to Government

A. The Christian and government.

1. (1-2) Government's legitimate authority and the Christian's response.

Let every soul be subject to the governing authorities. For there is no authority except from God, and the authorities that exist are appointed by God. Therefore whoever resists the authority resists the ordinance of God, and those who resist will bring judgment on themselves.

a. **Subject to the governing authorities**: The connection between Romans 12 and Romans 13 is clear. If the Christian is not to seek personal vengeance, it does not take away the government's authority to punish wrongdoers.

b. **Every soul**: This certainly includes Christians. Paul simply says that we should be **subject** to the governing authorities. This was in contrast to groups of zealous Jews in that day who recognized no king but God and paid taxes to no one but God.

c. **For there is no authority except from God, and the authorities that exist are appointed by God**: We subject ourselves to governing authorities because they are appointed by God and serve a purpose in His plan.

i. **No authority except from God**: God appoints a nation's leaders, but not always to *bless* the people. Sometimes it is to judge the people or to ripen the nation for judgment.

ii. We remember that Paul wrote this during the reign of the Roman Empire. It was no democracy, and no special friend to Christians - yet he still saw their legitimate authority.

iii. "Your Savior suffered under Pontius Pilate, one of the worst Roman governors Judea ever had; and Paul under Nero, the worst Roman Emperor. And neither our Lord nor His Apostle denied or reviled the 'authority!' " (Newell)

d. **Therefore whoever resists the authority resists the ordinance of God**: Since governments have authority from God, we are bound to obey them - unless, of course, they order us to do something in contradiction to God's law. Then, we are commanded to obey God before man (as in Acts 4:19).

e. **Those who resist will bring judgment on themselves**: God uses governing authorities as a check upon man's sinful desires and tendencies. Government can be an effective tool in resisting the effects of man's fallenness.

2. (3-4) The job of government: to punish and deter evildoers.

For rulers are not a terror to good works, but to evil. Do you want to be unafraid of the authority? Do what is good, and you will have praise from the same. For he is God's minister to you for good. But if you do evil, be afraid; for he does not bear the sword in vain; for he is God's minister, an avenger to *execute* wrath on him who practices evil.

a. **Do what is good, and you will have praise**: Paul's idea is that Christians should be the best citizens of all. Even though they are loyal to God before they are loyal to the state, Christians are good citizens because they are honest, give no trouble to the state, pay their taxes, and - most importantly - pray for the state and the rulers.

b. **He is God's minister**: Paul describes government officials as **God's minister**. They have a ministry in the plan and administration of God, just as much as church leaders do.

i. If the state's rulers are **God's minister** (servant), they should remember that they are *only* servants, and not gods themselves.

c. **An avenger to execute wrath on him who practices evil**: It is through the just punishment of evil that government serves its function in God's plan of holding man's sinful tendencies in check. When a government fails to do this consistently, it opens itself up to God's judgment and correction.

d. **He does not bear the sword in vain**: **The sword** is a reference to capital punishment. In the Roman Empire, criminals were typically executed by beheading with a **sword** (crucifixion was reserved for the worst criminals of the lowest classes). Paul, speaking by the inspiration of the Holy Spirit, has no doubt that the state has the legitimate authority to execute criminals.

3. (5-7) The Christian's responsibility towards government.

Therefore *you* must be subject, not only because of wrath but also for conscience' sake. For because of this you also pay taxes, for they are

God's ministers attending continually to this very thing. Render therefore to all their due: taxes to whom taxes *are due,* customs to whom customs, fear to whom fear, honor to whom honor.

a. **Therefore you must be subject**: We must be subject to government; not only because we fear punishment, but because we know it is right before God to do so.

i. **For conscience sake**: Christian obedience to the state is never blind - it obeys with the eyes of conscience wide open.

b. **You also pay taxes . . . Render therefore to all their due**: We are also to pay the taxes **due** from us, because there is a sense in which we support *God's work* when we do so.

i. By implication, Romans 13:6 also says that the taxes collected are to be used by government to get the job done of restraining evil and keeping an orderly society - not to enrich the government officials themselves.

c. **Taxes . . . customs . . . fear . . . honor**: We are to give to the state the money, honor, and proper reverence which are due to the state, all the while reserving our right to give to God that which is due to God alone (Matthew 22:21).

d. In light of this, is rebellion against government ever justified? If a citizen has a choice between two governments, it is right to choose and to promote the one that is most legitimate in God's eyes - the one which will best fulfill God's purpose for governments.

i. In a democracy we understand that there is a sense in which we *are* the government, and should not hesitate to help "govern" our democracy through our participation in the democratic process.

B. The Christian's obligation to his neighbors.

1. (8-10) The obligation to love.

Owe no one anything except to love one another, for he who loves another has fulfilled the law. For the commandments, "You shall not commit adultery," "You shall not murder," "You shall not steal," "You shall not bear false witness," "You shall not covet," and if *there is* any other commandment, are *all* summed up in this saying, namely, "You shall love your neighbor as yourself." Love does no harm to a neighbor; therefore love *is* the fulfillment of the law.

a. **Owe no one anything except to love one another**: On a personal level, the only "debt" we are to carry is the "debt" to love one another - this is a perpetual obligation we carry both before God and each other.

i. Some take this as a command to never borrow, but Jesus permitted borrowing in passages like Matthew 5:42. That isn't the sense of what Paul is saying here, though the Scriptures do remind us of the danger and obligations of borrowing (Proverbs 22:7).

ii. "We may pay our taxes and be quit. We may give respect and honor where they are due and have no further obligation. But we can never say, 'I have done all the loving I need to do.' Love then is a permanent obligation, a debt impossible to discharge." (Morris)

b. **You shall love your neighbor as yourself**: Paul echoes Jesus' words as recorded in Matthew 22:36-40. This is one of the two commands upon which *hang all the Law and the Prophets*.

i. **Love your neighbor** means to love the people you actually meet with and deal with every day. It is easy for us to love in the theoretical and the abstract, but God demands that we love *real* people.

ii. "No man can compass the ends of life by drawing a little line around himself upon the ground. No man can fulfill his calling as a Christian by seeking the welfare of his wife and family only, for these are only a sort of greater self." (Spurgeon)

c. **Love is the fulfillment of the law**: It is easy to do all the right religious "things" but to neglect love. Our love is the true measure of our obedience to God.

2. (11-14) The urgency to love and walk right with God.

And *do* this, knowing the time, that now *it is* high time to awake out of sleep; for now our salvation *is* nearer than when we *first* believed. The night is far spent, the day is at hand. Therefore let us cast off the works of darkness, and let us put on the armor of light. Let us walk properly, as in the day, not in revelry and drunkenness, not in lewdness and lust, not in strife and envy. But put on the Lord Jesus Christ, and make no provision for the flesh, to *fulfill its* lusts.

a. **The night is far spent, the day is at hand**: Because we know the danger of the times and we anticipate the soon return of Jesus, we should be all the more energetic and committed to a *right* walk with God instead of a *sleep-walk* with God.

i. How important it is to **awake out of sleep**! We can do many Christian things and essentially be asleep towards God. What a difference it makes when we are **awake**!

- We can speak when we are asleep
- We can hear when we are asleep
- We can walk when we are asleep

- We can sing when we are asleep
- We can think when we are asleep

b. **Cast off the works of darkness, and put on the armor of light**: The illustration is from taking off and putting on clothes. When you get dressed every day, you dress appropriately to who you are and what you plan to do. Therefore, everyday, **put on the Lord Jesus Christ**!

> i. We must **cast off** before we can **put on**. "The rags of sin must come off if we put on the robe of Christ. There must be a taking away of the love of sin, there must be a renouncing of the practices and habits of sin, or else a man cannot be a, Christian. It will be an idle attempt to try and wear religion as a sort of celestial overall over the top of old sins." (Spurgeon)

c. **The works of darkness**: These are characterized as **revelry and drunkenness, licentiousness and lust, strife and envy**. These are not appropriate for Christians who have come out of the night into God's light.

> i. The idea behind the word for **licentiousness** is "the desire for a forbidden bed." It describes the person who sets no value on sexual purity and fidelity.

> ii. **Lust** in this passage has the idea of people who are lost to shame. They no longer cares what people think and flaunt their sin openly, even proudly.

d. **The armor of light**: This is related to **the Lord Jesus Christ** Himself. When we put on Christ, we put on all the armor of God and are equipped to both defend and attack.

> i. "*Putting on Christ* is a strong and vivid metaphor. It means more than *put on the character of the Lord Jesus Christ*, signifying rather *Let Jesus Christ Himself be the armor that you wear.*" (Morris)

e. **Make no provision for the flesh**: The flesh will be as active as we allow it to be. We have a work to do in **walking properly, as in the day** - it isn't as if Jesus does it *for* us as we sit back; instead, He does it *through* us as we willingly and actively partner with Him.

> i. God used this passage to show Augustine, the great theologian of the early church, that he really *could* live the Christian life as empowered by the Holy Spirit - he just had to *do it*. And so do we.

Romans 14 - Helping a Weaker Brother

A. Don't judge each other in doubtful things.

1. (1-2) Receiving the weaker brother.

Receive one who is weak in the faith, *but* not to disputes over doubtful things. For one believes he may eat all things, but he who is weak eats *only* vegetables.

a. **Receive one who is weak in the faith**: We accept those weak in the faith, but not for the sake of carrying on a debate with them regarding **doubtful things**.

i. **Receive the one who is weak in the faith**: These are words to take seriously. Paul warns us to not make spiritual maturity a requirement for fellowship. We should distinguish between someone who is **weak** and someone who is *rebellious*.

ii. There are many reasons why a Christian might be weak.

- They may be a babe in Christ (babies are weak)
- They may be sick or diseased (by legalism)
- They may be malnourished (by lack of good teaching)
- They may lack exercise (needing exhortation)

b. **Eats only vegetables**: As an example of a *doubtful thing*, Paul looks at those who refuse to eat meat for a spiritual reason. Perhaps they refused it because they feared it was meat sacrificed to a pagan god (as in 1 Corinthians 8). Perhaps they refused the meat because it wasn't kosher, and they stuck to Jewish dietary regulations and traditions.

i. Because some Christian saw nothing wrong in this meat and others saw much wrong in it, this was a burning issue among believers in Paul's day. While the issue of not eating meat for spiritual reasons is no longer directly relevant to most Christians today, there are plenty of issues where some believers believe one way and others believe differently.

c. **He who is weak eats only vegetables**: In Paul's mind, the **weak** brother is the stricter one. It wasn't that they were weaker in their Christian life because of what they ate or didn't eat, but they were weaker because of their legalistic attitudes and lack of love towards others.

i. Undoubtedly these **weak** ones did not see themselves as weaker. It's likely they thought they were the strong ones, and the meat-eaters were the weak ones. Legalism has a way of making us think that we are strong and those who don't keep the rules the way we do are weak.

2. (3-4) Judging our brother is inappropriate because we are not their masters.

Let not him who eats despise him who does not eat, and let not him who does not eat judge him who eats; for God has received him. Who are you to judge another's servant? To his own master he stands or falls. Indeed, he will be made to stand, for God is able to make him stand.

a. **Let not him who eats despise him who does not eat**: It would be easy for a Christian who felt free to eat meat to **despise** others as hopeless legalists. It would also be easy for those who did not eat meat to **judge** those who did. But **God has received** those Christians who eat meat.

b. **Who are you to judge another's servant?** Paul reminds us that it isn't our place to pass judgment on any fellow Christian. They stand or fall before their own Master, God - and God is able to make those "meat eaters" stand.

i. There is a lot of useless, harmful division among Christians over silly, bigoted things. Paul isn't telling these Christians to *erase* their differences; he tells them to rise *above* them as Christian brothers and sisters.

3. (5-6) Judging our brother is inappropriate because these are matters of conscience.

One person esteems *one* day above another; another esteems every day *alike*. Let each be fully convinced in his own mind. He who observes the day, observes *it* to the Lord; and he who does not observe the day, to the Lord he does not observe *it*. He who eats, eats to the Lord, for he gives God thanks; and he who does not eat, to the Lord he does not eat, and gives God thanks.

a. **One person esteems one day above another; another esteems every day alike**: By bringing in the aspect of observing certain days, Paul lets us know that he is talking more about *principles* than *specific issues*. What he says has application to more than just eating meat.

b. **Let each be fully convinced in his own mind**: In such issues, Paul is willing to leave it up to the conscience of the individual. But whatever we do, we must be able to do it **to the Lord**, not using "conscience" as an excuse for obviously sinful behavior.

4. (7-9) We live and die to the Lord.

For none of us lives to himself, and no one dies to himself. For if we live, we live to the Lord; and if we die, we die to the Lord. Therefore, whether we live or die, we are the Lord's. For to this end Christ died and rose and lived again, that He might be Lord of both the dead and the living.

a. **For none of us lives to himself, and no one dies to himself**: We must understand that from beginning to end our life is connected to other lives. Paul reminds the Roman Christians that "No man is an island."

b. **Whether we live or die, we are the Lord's**: From beginning to end, our lives are to be dedicated to God. Therefore, whatever we do, we do it **to the Lord** - because Jesus *is* our Lord (**that He might be Lord of both the dead and the living**).

5. (10-12) Judging our brother is inappropriate because we will all face judgment before Jesus.

But why do you judge your brother? Or why do you show contempt for your brother? For we shall all stand before the judgment seat of Christ. For it is written: "As I live, says the LORD, every knee shall bow to Me, and every tongue shall confess to God." So then each of us shall give account of himself to God.

a. **But why do you judge your brother? Or why do you show contempt for your brother?** Probably, the use of both **judge** and **show contempt** is meant to have application to both the "strict" and the "free" individuals. In either case, the attitude is wrong because **we shall all stand before the judgment seat of Christ**.

i. The *strict* Christian found it easy to **judge** his brother, writing him off as an unspiritual meat-eater-compromiser. The *free* Christian found it easy to **show contempt** against his brother, regarding him as a uptight-legalistic-goody-good. Essentially, Paul's answer is "Stop worrying about your brother. You have enough to answer for before Jesus."

ii. **The judgment seat of Christ**: "This is the *bema* seat, equivalent to the judge's seat in the Olympic Games. After each game, the winners came before the judge's seat to receive crowns for first, second, and third places. Likewise, the Christian's works will be tested by fire, and he'll be rewarded for those which remain . . . The judgment seat of Christ is only concerned with a Christian's rewards and position in the kingdom, not with his salvation." (Smith)

b. **Every knee shall bow**: The quotation from Isaiah 45:23 emphasizes the fact that all will have to appear before God in humility, and **give account of himself before God**. If this is the case, we should let God deal with our brother.

6. (13) Summary: don't make it an issue of judging, but don't use your liberty to stumble another brother.

Therefore let us not judge one another anymore, but rather resolve this, not to put a stumbling block or a cause to fall in *our* brother's way.

a. **Let us not judge one another**: In the Sermon on the Mount, Jesus helped us to understand what this means - it means judging others according to a standard that we would not want to have applied to ourself.

i. This does not take away the need and the responsibility for admonishment (Romans 15:14) or rebuke (2 Timothy 4:2). When we admonish or rebuke, we do it over *clear Scriptural principles*, not over *doubtful things*. We may offer *advice* to others about doubtful things, but should never judge them.

b. **Not to put a stumbling block or a cause to fall in our brother's way**: We might stumble or cause our brother to fall in two ways. We can discourage or beat them down through our legalism against them, or we can do it by enticing them to sin through an unwise use of our liberty.

B. Don't stumble each other over doubtful things.

1. (14-15) Destroying a brother makes a privilege wrong.

I know and am convinced by the Lord Jesus that *there is* nothing unclean of itself; but to him who considers anything to be unclean, to him *it is* unclean. Yet if your brother is grieved because of *your* food, you are no longer walking in love. Do not destroy with your food the one for whom Christ died.

a. **I know and am convinced by the Lord Jesus that there is nothing unclean of itself**: Paul knew that there was nothing intrinsically unclean about meat that was not kosher or sacrificed to an idol. Yet there was *nothing* that could justify the destruction of a Christian brother over food.

i. Trapp on **I know and am convinced**: "Many, on the contrary, are persuaded before they know; and such will not be persuaded to know."

b. **You are no longer walking in love**: The issue now is not my personal liberty; it is **walking in love** towards one whom Jesus loves and died for.

c. **Do not destroy with your food the one for whom Christ died**: If Jesus was willing to give up His life for the sake of that brother, I can certainly give up my steak dinner.

2. (16-18) Pursuing the higher call of the Kingdom of God.

Therefore do not let your good be spoken of as evil; for the kingdom of God is not eating and drinking, but righteousness and peace and joy in the Holy Spirit. For he who serves Christ in these things *is* acceptable to God and approved by men.

a. **Do not let your good be spoken of as evil**: Our liberty in Jesus and freedom from the law is **good**, but not if we use it to destroy another brother in Christ. If we do that, then it could rightly be **spoken of as evil**.

b. **The kingdom of God is not eating and drinking**: If we place **food and drink** before **righteousness and peace and joy in the Holy Spirit**, then we are hopelessly out of touch with God's priorities and His heart.

c. **Acceptable to God and approved by men**: Serving God with a heart for His **righteousness and peace and joy** is the kind of service that is **acceptable** in His sight, and will be **approved by men**.

3. (19-21) Use your liberty to build each other up, not to tear each other down.

Therefore let us pursue the things *which make* for peace and the things by which one may edify another. Do not destroy the work of God for the sake of food. All things indeed *are* pure, but *it is* evil for the man who eats with offense. *It is* good neither to eat meat nor drink wine nor *do anything* by which your brother stumbles or is offended or is made weak.

a. **Do not destroy the work of God for the sake of food**: If eating or drinking something will stumble another brother, then we are not free to eat or drink in that circumstance. Even if we have the personal liberty, we do not have the liberty to stumble, offend, or weaken a brother.

b. **All things indeed are pure**: Paul will concede the point that there is nothing impure in the food itself; but he likewise insists that there is nothing pure in causing a brother to stumble.

c. **Nor do anything by which your brother stumbles or is offended or is made weak**: However, we shouldn't think that Paul would permit this kind of heart to cater to someone's legalism. Paul speaks about the stumbling of a sincere heart, not catering to the whims of someone's legalism.

i. For example, when some Christians from a Jewish background were offended that Gentile believers were not circumcised, Paul didn't cater to their legalistic demands.

4. (22-23) The concluding principle of faith.

Do you have faith? Have *it* to yourself before God. Happy *is* he who does not condemn himself in what he approves. But he who doubts is

condemned if he eats, because *he does* not *eat* from faith; for whatever *is* not from faith is sin.

a. **Do you have faith?** If you **have** [strong] **faith**, and feel liberty to partake of certain things, praise God! But have your strong faith **before God**, not before a brother who will stumble.

b. **Happy is he who does not condemn himself in what he approves**: Not every Christian knows this happiness. There are things God may challenge us to give up, but we go on approving them in our life - thus we **condemn ourselves**. It may not be that the thing itself is clearly good or bad, but it is enough that God speaks to us about the matter.

i. Each of us must ask: "God what is there in my life hindering a closer walk with You? I want to know the happiness that comes from not condemning myself by what I approve in my life." This takes faith, because we often cling to hindering things because we *think* they make us happy. Real happiness is found being closer and closer to Jesus, and by not being condemned by what we approve.

c. **Whatever is not from faith is sin**: Paul concludes with another principle by which we can judge "gray areas" - if we can't do it in faith, then it is sin.

i. This is a wonderful check on our tendency to justify ourselves in the things we permit. If we are troubled by something, it likely isn't **of faith** and likely **is sin** for us.

Romans 15 - Living to Bless Your Brother

A. Being filled in the Christian life.

1. (1-2) Filled with care and concern for others.

We then who are strong ought to bear with the scruples of the weak, and not to please ourselves. Let each of us please *his* neighbor for *his* good, leading to edification.

a. **We then who are strong ought to bear with the scruples of the weak, and not to please ourselves**: If you consider yourself strong in comparison to your brother, use your strength to serve your brothers in Christ - instead of using your "strength" just to please yourself.

i. **Bear with**: The idea isn't really bearing *with*, but bearing *up* the weaker brother - supporting him with your superior strength.

ii. This goes against the whole tenor of our times, which counsels people to "look out for number 1" and despises those who live lives of real sacrifice for the sake of others. Yet, undeniably Paul points the way to true happiness and fulfillment in life - get your eyes off of yourself, start building up others and you will find yourself built up.

b. **Let each of us please his neighbor**: It is a simple yet challenging call to simply put our neighbor first. Paul later wrote much the same thing in Philippians 2:3-4: *Let nothing be done through selfish ambition or conceit, but in lowliness of mind let each esteem others better than himself. Let each of you look out not only for his own interests, but also for the interests of others.*

i. This does not mean that the church is ruled by the whims of the weak. "A genuine concern for the weak will mean an attempt to make them strong by leading them out of their irrational scruples so that they, too, can be strong." (Morris)

c. **Let each of us please his neighbor for his good**: This shows that Paul does not mean being a "man-pleaser." Such a person may want to **please his neighbor**, but not **for his** neighbor's **good**.

d. **Leading to edification**: All too often, Christians find it easier to tear each other down instead of building each other up; this is a classic strategy of Satan against the church that must be resisted.

2. (3-4) Filled with the example of Jesus, who always put others first.

For even Christ did not please Himself; but as it is written, "The reproaches of those who reproached You fell on Me." For whatever things were written before were written for our learning, that we through the patience and comfort of the Scriptures might have hope.

a. **For even Christ did not please Himself**: Jesus is the ultimate example of one who did not **please Himself**, but put others first. Paul's classic development of this idea is in Philippians 2:5-11.

b. **As it is written**: As Jesus took abuse and suffered wrong for God's glory, He fulfilled what was written in God's word. Jesus showed by example that for the most part we are entirely too quick to vindicate ourselves, instead of letting God vindicate us. Jesus showed how the Father is well able to vindicate us.

c. **The reproaches of those who reproached You fell on Me**: The commandment Jesus fulfilled from Psalm 69:7 applies to us as well. It was **written for our learning**, that we **might have hope**, knowing we are doing what is right even when it is difficult.

i. When we respond rightly to the **reproaches** the world casts against us for Jesus' sake, it bothers them even more. It makes them know there isn't anything they can do against a child of God whose eyes are really on Jesus.

3. (5-6) A prayer for the fulfillment of this attitude in the Romans.

Now may the God of patience and comfort grant you to be like-minded toward one another, according to Christ Jesus, that you may with one mind *and* one mouth glorify the God and Father of our Lord Jesus Christ.

a. **Now may the God**: The fact that Paul puts these words into the form of a prayer demonstrates that he recognizes that this is a work that the Holy Spirit must do inside us.

b. **The God of patience**: Our God is a **God of patience**. We are often in such a hurry and God often seems to work too slowly for us. Often the purposes of God seem to be delayed but they always are fulfilled. God's delays are not His denials, and He has a loving purpose in every delay.

i. We *love* God's patience with His *people* - we need Him to be patient with us! Yet we often resent God's patience with His *plan* - we think He should hurry up. Nevertheless, God is patient both with His people and in His plan.

c. **That you may**: The goal is to **glorify the God and Father of our Lord Jesus Christ**. We accomplish that goal by having **one mind** and **one mouth** - by unity in our thinking and speech.

4. (7-13) Filled with love for others and joy and peace by the Holy Spirit.

Therefore receive one another, just as Christ also received us, to the glory of God. Now I say that Jesus Christ has become a servant to the circumcision for the truth of God, to confirm the promises *made* **to the fathers, and that the Gentiles might glorify God for** *His* **mercy, as it is written: "For this reason I will confess to You among the Gentiles, and sing to Your name." And again he says: "Rejoice, O Gentiles, with His people!" And again: "Praise the LORD, all you Gentiles! Laud Him, all you peoples!" And again, Isaiah says: "There shall be a root of Jesse; and He who shall rise to reign over the Gentiles, in Him the Gentiles shall hope." Now may the God of hope fill you with all joy and peace in believing, that you may abound in hope by the power of the Holy Spirit.**

a. **Therefore receive one another**: Instead of letting these issues about disputable things divide Christians (especially making a division between Jew and Gentile), we should receive one another just as Christ received us - in the terms of pure grace, knowing yet bearing with our faults.

i. Spurgeon on **just as Christ also received us**: "Christ did not receive us because we were perfect, because he could see no fault in us, or because he hoped to gain somewhat at our hands. Ah, no! But, in loving condescension covering our faults, and seeking our good, he welcomed us to his heart; so, in the same way, and with the same purpose, let us receive one another."

b. **As it is written**: Paul quotes a series of passages from the Old Testament demonstrating that God intends that the Gentiles praise Him. Instead of dividing over disputable matters, Jews and Gentiles should unite in Jesus over the common ground of praise.

i. **I will confess to You among the Gentiles**: The quotation from Psalm 18 describes Jesus Himself giving praise among the Gentiles.

c. **Now may the God of hope fill you with all joy and peace**: The prayer and blessing concluding the section is appropriate. As God fills us with the blessings of His **joy and peace in believing**, we are equipped to live in this common bond of unity God calls us to.

B. Paul's burden in ministry.

1. (14-16) Paul's reason for writing.

Now I myself am confident concerning you, my brethren, that you also are full of goodness, filled with all knowledge, able also to admonish one another. Nevertheless, brethren, I have written more boldly to you

on *some* points, as reminding you, because of the grace given to me by **God, that I might be a minister of Jesus Christ to the Gentiles, ministering the gospel of God, that the offering of the Gentiles might be acceptable, sanctified by the Holy Spirit.**

a. **Able also to admonish one another**: Paul didn't write because he felt the Roman Christians couldn't discern what was right before God or admonish each other to do right. Rather, he wrote to remind them, encouraging them to do what they knew was right.

b. **That I might be a minister of Jesus Christ to the Gentiles**: This is consistent with Paul's calling to **be a minister of Jesus Christ to the Gentiles**. In fulfilling this call, he didn't just preach the gospel of salvation but also instructed believers how to live before God.

c. **That the offering of the Gentiles might be acceptable**: When the Gentiles live glorifying God, then their **offering** to God is **acceptable, sanctified by the Holy Spirit** - the necessity of such a sacrifice makes Paul's writing necessary.

d. **The offering of the Gentiles**: Romans 15:16 is filled with the language of priesthood. Paul says he serves as a "ministering priest" of Jesus Christ presenting the gospel as a "priestly service" so Gentile converts would be an acceptable sacrifice to God.

i. "When he defines his ministry as *ministering the gospel of God* the apostle uses a word occurring nowhere else in the New Testament which may properly be rendered 'acting as a priest.' So the ministry of the gospel is conceived of after the pattern of priestly offering." (Murray)

2. (17-19) Paul glories in the work God has done through him.

Therefore I have reason to glory in Christ Jesus in the things *which pertain* to God. For I will not dare to speak of any of those things which Christ has not accomplished through me, in word and deed, to make the Gentiles obedient; in mighty signs and wonders, by the power of the Spirit of God, so that from Jerusalem and round about to Illyricum I have fully preached the gospel of Christ.

a. **Therefore I have reason to glory in Christ Jesus**: As he considers his call to be a **minister of Jesus Christ to the Gentiles,** Paul can glory in God that he received such a call - speaking only of the things God did through him to bring salvation to the Gentiles.

i. "Paul will glory only in what Christ has done through him. He is sure that Christ has done great things through him, and he is glad that he can draw attention to those things. But he is not trying to attract adulation. It is what Christ has done that is his theme." (Morris)

b. **In word and deed, to make the Gentiles obedient**: God used **mighty signs and wonders** and the broader **power of the Spirit of God** to help Paul **fully** preach the gospel of Christ everywhere he went - from Jerusalem to Illyricum.

> i. **I fully preached the gospel of Christ**: We sense that Paul would consider "bare" preaching, without the active and sometimes miraculous work of the Holy Spirit evident, to be less than **fully** preaching the gospel.

c. **From Jerusalem and round about to Illyricum I have fully preached the gospel**: **Illyricum** is modern Yugoslavia and Albania. This means that Paul's ministry spread from **Illyricum** in the west to Jerusalem in the east.

d. **Christ Jesus . . . God . . . Spirit of God**: Paul effortlessly weaves references to each member of the Trinity in Romans 15:16-19. Paul can't talk about God without recognizing His three Persons.

3. (20-21) Paul's desire to preach the gospel in new places.

And so I have made it my aim to preach the gospel, not where Christ was named, lest I should build on another man's foundation, but as it is written: "To whom He was not announced, they shall see; and those who have not heard shall understand."

a. **Not where Christ was named**: Paul did not want to **build on another man's foundation**. Rather he wanted to do pioneer work for the Lord - not because it was wrong or bad to continue the work begun through another man, but because there was so much to do on the frontiers.

b. **But as it is written**: Paul saw his pioneering heart as obedience to the Scriptures, fulfilling the passage he quotes from the Old Testament.

C. Paul's desire to come to Rome.

1. (22-24) Why Paul hasn't visited the Christians in Rome yet.

For this reason I also have been much hindered from coming to you. But now no longer having a place in these parts, and having a great desire these many years to come to you, whenever I journey to Spain, I shall come to you. For I hope to see you on my journey, and to be helped on my way there by you, if first I may enjoy your *company* for a while.

a. **For this reason I also have been much hindered**: It was his great desire to do pioneer work that **hindered** him from coming to the Romans, though he did desire to see them.

b. **Whenever I journey to Spain, I shall come to you**: Therefore, Paul supposes that he will visit the Romans on a future trip to Spain, where Paul will preach the gospel on the frontiers. Stopping off in Rome on the way, Paul anticipates that he can enjoy the support and fellowship of the Romans before he goes to preach the gospel in the regions beyond.

> i. Paul probably wanted Rome to be his base of operations for the western part of the empire, even as Antioch was his base for the eastern part.

c. **For I hope to see you on my journey**: Paul had these plans; yet things did not work out according to his plans. He did go to Rome, yet not as a missionary on his way to Spain. He went to Rome as a prisoner awaiting trial before Caesar, where he would preach the gospel on a different kind of frontier.

> i. God had unexpected frontiers for the gospel in Paul's life, giving him unexpected access to preach to the emperor of Rome himself.

> ii. After his release from the Roman imprisonment at the end of the Book of Acts, we have reason to believe that Paul did in fact make it to Spain and preached the gospel there.

2. (25-29) Paul's present plans.

But now I am going to Jerusalem to minister to the saints. For it pleased those from Macedonia and Achaia to make a certain contribution for the poor among the saints who are in Jerusalem. It pleased them indeed, and they are their debtors. For if the Gentiles have been partakers of their spiritual things, their duty is also to minister to them in material things. Therefore, when I have performed this and have sealed to them this fruit, I shall go by way of you to Spain. But I know that when I come to you, I shall come in the fullness of the blessing of the gospel of Christ.

a. **But now I am going to Jerusalem to minister to the saints**: Paul thought he would stop in Corinth on his way to Jerusalem to deliver a collection from Christians in Macedonia and Achaia (Acts 20:1-3).

b. **For if the Gentiles have been partakers of their spiritual things, their duty is also to minister to them in material things**: Paul's observation is appropriate: the Gentile Christians of the broader Roman empire had received so much spiritually from the community of Jewish Christians in Jerusalem, it was only right that they help the Jerusalem Christians in their need.

c. **I shall go by way of you to Spain**: Paul would indeed head for Rome after his time in Jerusalem, but not in the way he planned!

3. (30-33) Paul's plea for prayer.

Now I beg you, brethren, through the Lord Jesus Christ, and through the love of the Spirit, that you strive together with me in prayers to

God for me, that I may be delivered from those in Judea who do not believe, and that my service for Jerusalem may be acceptable to the saints, that I may come to you with joy by the will of God, and may be refreshed together with you. Now the God of peace *be* with you all. Amen.

a. **Strive together with me in prayers to God for me, that I may be delivered from those in Judea who do not believe**: Sensing that danger awaited him in Jerusalem (having been warned several times as recorded in Acts 20:22-23 and Acts 21:10-14), Paul knew he needed the prayers of God's people to see him through the difficulty promised him.

i. **Strive together with me**: The idea is that Paul wants the Romans to partner with him in ministry through their prayers. The New English Bible translates this: *be my allies in the fight*. The New Living Bible translates the phrase like this: *join me in my struggle by praying to God for me*.

ii. "Ministers need the prayers of their flocks. With Paul I urge you to strive in your prayers for your pastors. We need your prayers and we thank God for them. Pastors are sustained by the power of the Spirit through the support of their congregations." (Smith)

iii. The ancient Greek word translated **strive together** is *sunagonizomai* - literally meaning, "agonize together." To emphasize the importance and intensity, Paul repeats the word twice: *sunagonizomai sunagonizomai*.

iv. This same root word for *agony* is used of Jesus' anguished prayer in the Garden of Gethsemane when Jesus asked His disciples to agonize with Him in prayer. They failed at that critical moment and left Jesus to struggle alone. We must not leave our ministers and leaders to struggle alone. "It reminds us of Carey, who says, when he goes to India, 'I will go down into the pit, but brother Fuller and the rest of you must hold the rope.' Can we refuse the request? Would it not be treachery?" (Spurgeon)

v. "Does it astonish you that a man so rich in grace as Paul should be asking prayers of these unknown saints? It need not astonish you; for it is the rule with the truly great to think most highly of others. In proportion as a man grows in grace he feels his dependence upon God, and, in a certain sense, his dependence upon God's people." (Spurgeon)

b. **That I may be delivered from those in Judea who do not believe**: Paul knew that his danger in Jerusalem would come from those who **did not believe**. This was the case, as demonstrated in Acts 21:27-28 and 22:22.

c. **And that my service for Jerusalem may be acceptable to the saints**: Paul knew that the church in Jerusalem was very conservative, and sometimes regarded men like Paul as dangerous innovators; for this reason, he asks the Romans to pray that **my service for Jerusalem may be acceptable to the saints**.

d. **That I may come to you with joy**: The prayers of Paul and the Romans were answered, though not in the manner they expected. Acts 28:15 describes Paul's "triumphal entry" into Rome, so that he did come to them **with joy** - though also in chains!

e. **Amen**: Paul concludes the letter here except for the personal greetings in   Romans 16.

Romans 16 - Greetings to the Christians in Rome

A. Greetings to many different Christians.

1. (1-2) A recommendation of Phoebe.

I commend to you Phoebe our sister, who is a servant of the church in Cenchrea, that you may receive her in the Lord in a manner worthy of the saints, and assist her in whatever business she has need of you; for indeed she has been a helper of many and of myself also.

a. **I commend to you Phoebe our sister**: Paul certainly knew the value of what women could do in serving the church. Apparently Phoebe was on her way to Rome (probably entrusted with this precious letter) and Paul sends an advance recommendation of this sister in Christ so the Romans will receive her and support her during her stay in their city.

b. **I commend to you**: Such recommendations were important because there was both great legitimate need for this kind of assistance and there were many deceivers who wanted to take advantage of the generosity of Christians.

c. **Phoebe**: This name is the feminine form of a title given to the pagan god Apollo, the title meaning "the bright one." Christians, on their conversion, seemed to feel no need to change their names even if there was some pagan significance to their name.

d. **Servant** is the same word translated *deacon* in other places. Phoebe seems to be a female deacon in the church, either by formal recognition or through her general service.

e. **She has been a helper of many and of myself also**: Paul gives Phoebe one of the best compliments anyone can give. This sort of practical help is essential in doing the business of the gospel.

2. (3-5a) Greetings to Priscilla and Aquilla.

Greet Priscilla and Aquila, my fellow workers in Christ Jesus, who risked their own necks for my life, to whom not only I give thanks, but

also all the churches of the Gentiles. Likewise *greet* the church that is in their house.

> a. **Priscilla and Aquila**: This couple is mentioned in Acts 18:2, 18:18 and 18:26 as associates of Paul and helpers to Apollos. Apparently they were now back in the city of Rome.
>
> > i. Spurgeon on **Priscilla and Aquila**: "When two loving hearts pull together they accomplish wonders. What different associations cluster around the names of 'Priscilla and Aquila' from those which are awakened by the words 'Ananias and Sapphira'! There we have a husband and a wife conspiring in hypocrisy, and here a wife and a husband united in sincere devotion."
>
> b. **The church that is in their house**: This phrase gives us a clue to the organization of the early church. In a city with a Christian community of any size, there would be several "congregations" meeting in different houses, since there were no "church" buildings at this time. Each house church probably had its own "pastor."

3. (5b-16) Various greetings.

Greet my beloved Epaenetus, who is the firstfruits of Achaia to Christ. Greet Mary, who labored much for us. Greet Andronicus and Junia, my countrymen and my fellow prisoners, who are of note among the apostles, who also were in Christ before me. Greet Amplias, my beloved in the Lord. Greet Urbanus, our fellow worker in Christ, and Stachys, my beloved. Greet Apelles, approved in Christ. Greet those who are of the *household* of Aristobulus. Greet Herodion, my countryman. Greet those who are of the *household* of Narcissus who are in the Lord. Greet Tryphena and Tryphosa, who have labored in the Lord. Greet the beloved Persis, who labored much in the Lord. Greet Rufus, chosen in the Lord, and his mother and mine. Greet Asyncritus, Phlegon, Hermas, Patrobas, Hermes, and the brethren who are with them. Greet Philologus and Julia, Nereus and his sister, and Olympas, and all the saints who are with them. Greet one another with a holy kiss. The churches of Christ greet you.

> a. **Epaenetus**: This man is of note because he was apparently among the very first converts of Achaia (where Corinth was and where Paul wrote the letter to the Romans). **Epaenetus** was also apparently dear to Paul; **beloved** isn't a term Paul used cheaply.
>
> b. **Andronicus and Junia**: These were apparently Jews (**my kinsmen**) and were imprisoned for the sake of the gospel (**my fellow prisoners**). They were well regarded **among the apostles**, having become Christians even before Paul did (sometime in the first 3 or 4 years after Pentecost).

i. **Of note among the apostles** has the idea that Andronicus and Junia are apostles themselves (though not of the twelve), and notable among other apostles. If there ever were women recognized as apostles - in the sense of being special emissaries of God, not in the sense of being of the twelve - this is the strongest Scriptural evidence. It isn't very strong.

c. **Amplias**: There is a tomb dating from the late first or early second century in the earliest Christian catacomb of Rome which bears the name AMPLIAS. Some suggest that this is the same person mentioned in Romans 16:8.

d. **Greet those who are of the household of Aristobulus**: The fact that the **household of Aristobulus** is greeted but not Aristobulus himself made Spurgeon think that Aristobulus was not converted but many in his **household** were. It made Spurgeon think of the unconverted who live with believers in their house.

i. "Where are you, Aristobulus? That is not your name, perhaps, but your character is the same as that of this unregenerate Roman, whose family knew the Lord. I might speak in God's name good words and comfortable words to your wife and to your children, but I could not so speak to you, Aristobulus! The Lord sends a message of grace to your dear child, to your beloved wife, but not to you; for you have not given your heart to him." (Spurgeon)

e. **Rufus**: This may be the same man mentioned as a son of Simon the Cyrene in Mark 15:21. This is possible, but **Rufus** was a common name - so it may have been someone else.

i. **Chosen in the Lord** has the idea that **Rufus** had some eminence among the Christians of Rome. It doesn't refer to his election in Jesus.

f. **Nereus**: In 95 A.D. two distinguished Romans were condemned for being Christians. The husband was executed and the wife was banished. The name of their chief servant was Nereus - this may be the same **Nereus** mentioned here and he may be the one who brought the gospel to them.

g. **Asyncritus . . . Phlegon . . . Patrobas . . . Hermes**: Of the rest of these names, Paul finds something wonderful to say about almost every one of them - noting their labor, his special regard for them (**beloved**), their standing in the Lord (**approved in Christ . . . in the Lord . . . chosen in the Lord**).

i. This is a tremendous example. It shows Paul's way of casting about uplifting words to build up God's people. He was generous in paying compliments that were both sincere and wonderful.

h. **Greet one another with a holy kiss**: This might sound strange to us, but Luke 7:45 shows how common a greeting a kiss was. Jesus rebukes a Pharisee because he did not give Jesus a kiss when He came into his house.

i. It seems that this practice was later abused. Clement of Alexandria complained about churches where people made the church resound with kissing, and says that "the shameless use of a kiss occasions foul suspicions the evil reports."

4. The value of Paul's extensive greetings to the Roman church.

a. Leon Morris explains that this section demonstrates that the Letter to the Romans "was a letter to real people and, as far as we can see, ordinary people; it was not written to professional theologians."

i. "They were like the most of us, commonplace individuals; but they loved the Lord, and therefore as Paul recollected their names he sent them a message of love which has become embalmed in the Holy Scriptures. Do not let us think of the distinguished Christians exclusively so as to forget the rank and file of the Lord's army. Do not let the eye rest exclusively upon the front rank, but let us love all whom Christ loves; let us value all Christ's servants. It is better to be God's dog than to be the devil's darling." (Spurgeon)

b. Notice the women mentioned in this chapter: **Phoebe, Priscilla, Mary, Tryphena, Tryphosa**, the mother of **Rufus**, and **Julia**. These are women who worked for the Lord.

i. "Ministry in the Spirit by a woman is different altogether from her taking over authority, or infringing upon the order of the assembly of God." (Newell)

c. Notice their work for the Lord: some, like **Tryphena and Tryphosa, labored in the Lord**. Others, like **Persis, labored much for the Lord**. "So there are distinctions and degrees in honor among believers, and these are graduated by the scale of service done. It is an honor to labor for Christ, it is a still greater honor to labor much. If, then, any, in joining the Christian church, desire place or position, honor or respect, the way to it is this - labor, and labor much." (Spurgeon)

d. Of the 24 names here, 13 also appear in inscriptions or documents connected with the Emperor's palace in Rome. We know that there were Christians among Caesar's household (Philippians 4:22). Paul may be writing many of the servants who worked for Caesar who became Christians.

B. Concluding words and warnings.

1. (17-20) A word of warning regarding dividers and deceivers.

Now I urge you, brethren, note those who cause divisions and offenses, contrary to the doctrine which you learned, and avoid them. For those

who are such do not serve our Lord Jesus Christ, but their own belly, and by smooth words and flattering speech deceive the hearts of the simple. For your obedience has become known to all. Therefore I am glad on your behalf; but I want you to be wise in what is good, and simple concerning evil. And the God of peace will crush Satan under your feet shortly. The grace of our Lord Jesus Christ *be* with you. Amen.

a. **Note those who cause divisions and offenses**: This has in mind both those who would *divide* God's people (**cause divisions**) and those who would *deceive* God's people (**offenses . . . contrary to the doctrine you have learned**). Once these have been *noted* (marked), they are to be *avoided*.

i. This is essential to God's purpose for the church. Truth without unity leads to pride; unity without truth leads to a departure from the true gospel itself. Each of these must be guarded against.

ii. **Now I urge you, brethren**: The tone here suggests how important this was to Paul; "It may well be that Paul took the pen and wrote these words himself . . . It is quite possible that Paul wrote these words, then passed the pen back to Tertius for a postscript. Something unusual happened at the end of this letter, and this is a very possible understanding of it." (Morris)

iii. "Mad dogs are shot; infectious diseases are quarantined; but evil teachers who would divide to their destruction and draw away the saints with teaching *contrary to the doctrine* of Christ and His Apostles are everywhere tolerated!" (Newell)

b. **By smooth words and flattering speech deceive**: The warning is necessary because these dividers and deceivers do not announce themselves. They use **smooth words and flattering speech** and always target **the simple** - usually those who are young in the faith.

i. **Deceive the hearts of the simple**: This shows that dividers and deceivers don't affect *everyone*. We must not wait until *everyone* is scattered or deceived until we are concerned with dividers and deceivers.

c. **Do not serve our Lord Jesus Christ, but their own belly**: Dividers and deceivers never *want* to appear selfish. Typically they perceive themselves as noble crusaders for a great cause. Nevertheless, however they may appear on the outside, their motives are essentially selfish and fleshly.

d. **Your obedience has become known to all**: This means that when it comes to dividers and deceivers, it isn't that the Romans must correct a bad situation. They are already dealing with these situations well, and Paul is **glad** about it. Yet they must remain diligent against the attacks of the dividers and the deceivers.

e. **Be wise in what is good**: This is the best defense against dividers and deceivers. It is of far more use to know the good than it is to know the evil, to learn about the genuine rather than the counterfeit.

f. **The God of peace will crush Satan under your feet shortly**: Any church with the well-deserved reputation of the Romans, who stays on guard against both dividers and deceivers, will see God **crush Satan under your feet shortly**.

> i. We see that God does the crushing, but Satan ends up under the feet of believers.

> ii. Of course, this will not ultimately happen until Satan is bound and cast into the bottomless pit (Revelation 20:1-3); but every victory God wins for us right now is a preview of that event.

2. (21-24) Greetings from those in Corinth with Paul.

Timothy, my fellow worker, and Lucius, Jason, and Sosipater, my countrymen, greet you. I, Tertius, who wrote *this* epistle, greet you in the Lord. Gaius, my host and *the host* of the whole church, greets you. Erastus, the treasurer of the city, greets you, and Quartus, a brother. The grace of our Lord Jesus Christ *be* with you all. Amen.

a. **Timothy** rightly rates a first mention, being one of Paul's closest and most trusted associates.

b. **I, Tertius, who wrote this epistle: Tertius** was Paul's writer as the apostle dictated the letter. This was Paul's normal practice in writing letters to churches, but this is the only letter where Paul's secretary is mentioned by name.

c. **Gaius**: This brother had such a reputation for hospitality that Paul can say he was regarded as **the host of the whole church**.

3. (25-27) Conclusion to the letter: praise to God.

Now to Him who is able to establish you according to my gospel and the preaching of Jesus Christ, according to the revelation of the mystery kept secret since the world began but now has been made manifest, and by the prophetic Scriptures has been made known to all nations, according to the commandment of the everlasting God, for obedience to the faith; to God, alone wise, *be* glory through Jesus Christ forever. Amen.

a. **Now to Him who is able**: With all the dangers facing the Romans - and every church - Paul fittingly concludes by commending them to **Him who is able to establish you**. Paul also knows that this will be done **according to my gospel and the preaching of Jesus Christ**.

b. **According to the revelation of the mystery**: Paul means this as the whole plan of redemption through Jesus Christ. Though God announced much of the plan previously through prophecy, its final outworking wasn't evident until revealed by God through Jesus.

i. Now that the **mystery** has been revealed through the preaching of the gospel, God calls **all nations to obedience to the faith**.

c. **To God, alone wise, be glory through Jesus Christ forever**: In this conclusion Paul reflects on the wisdom of God's plan in the gospel and the fact that such wisdom is beyond man. God had a plan no man would come up with, but the wisdom and glory of the plan is evident.

i. If there is anything that the Book of Romans explains from beginning to end, it is the *greatness* and *glory* of this plan of God that Paul preached as a *gospel* - as good news. It's entirely fitting that Paul concludes this letter praising the God of such a gospel.

ii. The good news Paul preached presented the God who chose to glorify Himself through the person and work of Jesus Christ, and who will glorify Himself that way **forever. Amen!**

Romans - Bibliography

This is a bibliography of books cited in the commentary. Of course, there are many other worthy works on the Book of Romans, but these are listed for the benefit of readers who wish to check sources.

Barclay, William *The Letter to the Romans* (Philadelphia: Westminster Press, 1975)

Bruce, F.F. *The Letter of Paul to the Romans* (Grand Rapids, Michigan: Eerdmans, 1988)

Calvin, John *Commentaries on the Epistle of Paul to the Romans* (Grand Rapids, Michigan: Baker Book House, 1979)

Chrysostom, John *Homilies on the Epistle to the Romans* (Grand Rapids, Michigan: Eerdmans, 1980, from *The Nicene and Post-Nicene Fathers, Volume XI*)

Clarke, Adam *The New Testament with A Commentary and Critical Notes, Volume II* (New York: Eaton & Mains, 1831)

Fry, William Francis *Notes and Outlines of the Books of the Bible* (Lubbock, Texas: Baptist Bible Chair, 1940)

Harrison, Everett F. Romans, *The Expositor's Bible Commentary, Volume 10* (Grand Rapids, Michigan: Zondervan, 1976)

Landis, Benson Y. *An Outline of the Bible, Book by Book* (New York: Barnes and Noble, 1963)

Lenski, R.C.H. *The Interpretation of St. Paul's Epistle to the Romans* (Minneapolis, Minnesota: Augsburg, 1961)

Luther, Martin *Commentary on the Epistle to the Romans* (Grand Rapids, Michigan: Zondervan, 1954)

Maclaren, Alexander *Expostions of Holy Scripture, Volume Twelve* (Grand Rapids, Michigan: Baker, 1984)

Meyer, F.B. *Our Daily Homily* (Westwood, New Jersey: Fleming H. Revell Company, 1966)

Morgan, G. Campbell *An Exposition of the Whole Bible* (Old Tappan, New Jersey: Fleming H. Revell Company, 1959)

Morgan, G. Campbell *Handbook for Bible Teachers and Preachers* (Grand Rapids, Michigan: Baker Book House, 1982)

Morgan, G. Campbell *Searchlights from the Word* (New York: Fleming H. Revell Company, 1926)

Morris, Leon *The Epistle to the Romans* (Grand Rapids, Michigan: Eerdmans, 1988)

Murray, John *The Epistle to the Romans* (Grand Rapids, Michigan: Eerdmans, 1987)

Newell, William R. *Romans Verse by Verse* (Chicago: Moody Press, 1979)

Poole, Matthew *A Commentary on the Holy Bible, Volume III: Matthew-Revelation* (London: Banner of Truth Trust, 1969, first published in 1685)

Smith, Chuck *The Gospel According to Grace* (Costa Mesa, California: The Word for Today, 1981)

Spurgeon, Charles Haddon *The New Park Street Pulpit, Volumes 1-6* and *The Metropolitan Tabernacle Pulpit, Volumes 7-63* (Pasadena, Texas: Pilgrim Publications, 1990)

Trapp, John *A Commentary on the Old and New Testaments, Volume Five* (Eureka, California: Tanski Publications, 1997)

Wiersbe, Warren W. *The Bible Exposition Commentary Volume 1* (Wheaton, Illinios: Victor Books, 1989)

Wuest, Kenneth *Romans In the Greek New Testament* (Grand Rapids, Michigan: Eerdmans, 1973)

Much thanks to the many who helped prepare this commentary. My wife Inga-Lill and our children give so much support in this and all the ministry. Tim and Martina Patrick's friendship is a special gift through the years and Martina worked long and hard proof-reading and making me look like a better writer than I really am Thanks, Martina! Craig Brewer created the cover and helped with the layout. Kara Valeri helped with graphic design. Gayle Erwin provided both inspiration and practical guidance. I am often amazed at the remarkable kindness of others, and thanks to all who give the gift of encouragement. With each year that passes, faithful friends and supporters become all the more precious. Through you all, God has been better to me than I have ever deserved.

David Guzik is the Pastor of Calvary Chapel of Simi Valley. David and his wife Inga-Lill live in Simi Valley with their children Aan-Sofie, Nathan, and Jonathan. You can e-mail David at davidguzik@calvarychapel.com

For more resources by David Guzik, go to www.enduringword.com

More Bible Study Resources
from Enduring Word Media

Ask for these works from your local Christian bookstore,
or order directly from Enduring Word Media.

Books - Bible Commentary

Genesis (ISBN: 1-56599-049-8)
Acts (ISBN: 1-56599-047-1)
First Corinthians (ISBN: 1-56599-045-5)
Second Corinthians (ISBN: 1-56599-042-0)
Revelation (ISBN: 1-56599-043-9)

Software - CD-ROM

New Testament & More (ISBN: 1-56599-048-X)

This CD-ROM gives immediate access to thousands of pages of verse-by-verse Bible commentary through all of the New Testament and many Old Testament books. For ease of use, commentary is available in both Acrobat and HTML format. Also includes bonus audio resources - hours of David Guzik's teaching in mp3 format

Enduring Word Media

www.enduringword.com • ewm@enduringword.com
23 West Easy Street, #204 • Simi Valley, CA 93065
(805) 582-6545